How to Get Rich

Rich

Secret to Financial Stability and Easy Tips

(Unleash the Things That Wise and Rich People Do)

Philip White

Published By **Andrew Zen**

Philip White

How to Get Rich: Secret to Financial Stability and Easy Tips (Unleash the Things That Wise and Rich People Do)

ISBN   978-1-998927-60-9

No part of this guidebook shall be reproduced in any form without permission in writing from the publisher except in the case of brief quotations embodied in critical articles or reviews.

Legal & Disclaimer

Table Of Contents

Chapter 1: Financial Services.................... 1

Chapter 2: Accounting 11

Chapter 3: Automotive Manufacturing .. 20

Chapter 4: Infrastructure & Energy 33

Chapter 5: Healthcare 42

Chapter 6: Government & Public
Information... 50

Chapter 7: Retail & Cpg......................... 56

Chapter 8: Information & Conversation . 69

Chapter 9: Enterprise Tech 88

Chapter 10: How To Build Wealth.......... 96

Chapter 11: The Price Of Stepped Forward
Connectivity 112

Chapter 12: Dominating The Game Of
Wealth 123

Chapter 13: The Mindset Of The Rich .. 130

Chapter 14: Rich People Generally Think
Northward 133

Chapter 15: Befriend Money................ 140

Chapter 16: The Rich Create Open Doors
Thump At Their Door 146

Chapter 17: Get Rich: Yes You Can 155

Chapter 18: The Road To Riches........... 161

Chapter 19: Get Rich: Tips For Success. 167

Chapter 20: Staying Rich: What It Takes To
Maintain Your Wealth.......................... 175

Chapter 21: Richest People In The World
.... 179

Chapter 22: Getting Rich: The Bottom Line
.... 182

Chapter 1: Financial services

Banking

This is absolutely the begin of what is to are to be had terms of blockchain and banking. Banks act as crucial price storage and transmission centres from a macroeconomic point of view. Blockchains might also enhance accuracy and statistics transmission inside the monetary offerings company by using the use of serving as digital, solid, and tamper-evidence ledgers. JPMorgan Chase has released the JPM Coin on the blockchain to simplify move-border bills amongst its organization clients in actual-time. Goldman Sachs and Citigroup are different economic establishments that have dabbled with blockchain generation. The incumbents utilised Axoni's Axcore blockchain in February 2020 to perform an equity transfer. "Blockchain has the capability to disrupt the $five trillion-plus banking industry by way of way of crucial disintermediating offerings furnished by way of banks, which includes bills and clearing and settlement structures." Banks make severa money through facilitating payments, and Juniper Research estimates that B2B move-border transactions will exceed $35 trillion in fee via 2022. While traditional banking is based on 0.33 events to verify the authenticity of a transaction, blockchain generation gets rid of this step while providing a faster and similarly constant technique of turning in coins. B2B global bypass-border blockchain payments will rise from 122 million in 2020 to over 1.Eight billion through 2025. Ripple, a blockchain commercial business corporation, has labored with extra than 300 clients, along side economic institutions like Santander and Western Union, to beautify circulate-border bills overall performance. RippleNet makes use of a decentralised infrastructure to deliver global bills in 3 seconds in desire to the 5 days it may take for normal international economic organization transfers. RippleNet bills. In a a success trial, Switzerland's crucial economic institution hired R3, a key leader in allocated ledger technology for banks, to settle enormous transactions amongst monetary establishments using virtual overseas money.

Stock buying and selling & hedge fee variety

New blockchain-centered groups are really trying to automate and guard the technique more effectively than any previous solution after years of companies operating to simplify stock looking for, promoting, and buying and selling. Overstock's parent organisation, Trades on T.Com, may be accomplished the use of blockchain technology. Incorporating cryptographically strong disbursed ledgers into the conventional shopping for and selling device the use of the tZERO platform improves transparency and audibility. A shorter agreement time is each specific purpose of Credit Suisse. For the primary time in April

2021, it settledinventory gives at the identical day, one at eleven a.M. ET and the possibility at three p.M. ET. At 4:30 p.M. Eastern Time, a agreement modified into reached via the Paxos Settlement Service. For blockchain to benefit traction, it ought to form alliances with exceptional trade networks and exchanges. Since its acquisition by means of using Stellar in 2018, Chain, a blockchain startup, has been instrumental in orchestrating a a achievement stay blockchain integration between the Nasdaq stock marketplace and Citi's banking infrastructure.

More currently, Nasdaq teamed up with R3 to offer a platform for financial establishments to assemble and run their digital asset exchanges, using R3's organization blockchain software program software program, Corda. Numerai, however, is adopting the hedge fund idea and decentralising it via hiring many investors and quants. With the backing of

4

First Round Capital and Union Square Ventures, the Numerai platform encrypts statistics and invitations its loads of different quantitative analysts to bring together predictive fashions. Numerai's cryptocurrency token, Numeraire, is presented to the exceptional participants. For this cause, Numerai affords a meta-model for getting and promoting. It modified into said in October of 2020 that the Numerai Signals mission, which can take indicators from fashions knowledgeable on datasets apart from the organization's, will begin in November of the same yr. "The maximum progressive signs" may be rewarded with the enterprise's $50 million surely worth of Numeraire tokens. According to the platform's maximum current quarterly document, tokens sincerely really worth $28 million had been staked as of Q3'21, and Numeraire stakes had decrease returned 15 consistent with cent over the preceding 3 months. Soon, impact investment will enjoy the usage of blockchain generation and gather the United Nations' Sustainable Development Goals; effect tokens may be used. Integrated with smart contracts, the ones tokens may be used as a shape of fee or praise. They may be used for a variety of things. It is common to schooling dispensing Collaboration Impact Tokens to site site visitors who visit a lot less-well-known locations to alleviate congestion in more famous ones. Governments may also use the ones tokens to manipulate traveler waft better. HARA tokens encourage farmers to proportion and verify agricultural facts with the resource of providing a reward for every a hit information sharing and verification.

Crowdfunding

There is a herbal healthful between crowdfunding and blockchain competencies due to the reality supporters (aka "pledgers") or man or woman traders can also additionally without delay finance inventors and entrepreneurs, thereby "disintermediating" capital creation logo have end up the primary crucial feature film to be subsidized using a token "crowd sale" at the Ethereum blockchain with a $1.4 million advertising and marketing advertising marketing campaign on Weifund. The film changed into created or maybe tested on the Tribeca Film Festival to especially excellent evaluations, however investors' cash remains unknown. The Initial Coin Offerings (ICOs) approach, similar to a publicly-traded enterprise's inventory sale but makes use of blockchain generation, is each distinctive form of blockchain-powered crowdfunding. Cooperation amongst Protocol Labs and AngelList, like CoinList, brings virtual property to the general public thru helping blockchain institutions create criminal and compliant token services. Two distinctive businesses are growing in the ICO atmosphere: Waves, a platform for the garage, manage, and issuance of digital property, and Republic, a crypto initiative that permits customers to participate in

ICOs for as low as $10 constant with transaction. Waves. Unlike Kickstarter and Indiegogo, Pledgecamp attempts to sell transparency and provide "Backer Insurance" thru decentralising the device. Escrow charge range are held in a wallet for safety till the challenge's funding reason is attained. Investors can screen the task's development and function a say in its future route, as an example, by using the use of voting on whether or not or not the project need to pass right right into a present day phase.

Crypto exchanges

By casting off human intermediaries, blockchain minimises the risk of hacking, corruption, or a human mistake, reducing conventional cybersecurity hazard. Ironically, some of the maximum a success blockchain organizations are intermediaries with a excessive diploma of centralisation. New ventures are "dogfooding" the exchange of blockchain-primarily based clearly currencies via posting the whole transaction at the blockchain. To name absolutelyoutstanding backers, Enigma counts MIT and Flybridge Capital among its ranks. Enigma advanced a decentralised trade and making an investment platform that does not rely on a 3rd celebration to feature as a clearinghouse is being developed thru Enigma, and it's far called Catalyst.0x, an Ethereum-based decentralised change one of the maximum famous. Binance and Coinbase,well-known centralised exchanges, have made inroads into the decentralised exchange market thru beginning Binance DEX and buying the-to-peer buying and promoting platform Paradex, respectively.

Wills & inheritances

A blockchain clever settlement answer is right for wills given that they may be a totally specialised form of settlement. It is commonplace for will-related litigation to embody disturbing situations to the "genuineness" of a will—that is, whether or not or no longer the crook interpretation is steady with the vain's intentions—along proving that the deceased died. Even at the same time as blockchain era couldn't alleviate the ones disturbing situations, it might make figuring out right data, presenting verifiable transaction information, and debunking faux claims a lot less tough. For folks that need to keep away from probate and crook disputes over the validity of an inheritance remember, Japan-based totally completely totally enterprise Zweispace is operating on a self-executing will device the usage of a blockchain that might robotically transfer assets of a receive as proper with to beneficiaries while the trustee passes away.

Chapter 2: Accounting

It's only a do not forget of time until accountants have a look at match.

Tax papers, financial institution statements, and spreadsheets are clearly some of the every day office paintings that accountants deal with. Blockchain technology would possibly assist accounting companies higher show this non-public information as it's miles treated.

To eliminate human mistakes and fraud, blockchain generation also can help in automating sure accounting functions the usage of AI.

Early adopters encompass the Big Four accounting organizations. EY's Blockchain Analyzer can help auditors in efficaciously vetting digital property, while KPMG has engaged in programmes and tasks to explore and disseminate knowledge on the blockchain. PwC has built an auditing company for bitcoin assets.

Loans & credit

Traditional banks and lenders underwrite loans based totally on a device of credit score rating reporting. Using a credit rating record issued with the useful resource of 1 in each of 3 crucial credit score businesses — Experian, TransUnion, and Equifax — banks test the chance that you obtained't pay them lower lower back. This centralized structure is probably hostile to clients. The Federal Trade Commission (FTC) believes that extra than a third of Americans have a "doubtlessly exquisite errors" in their credit rating rating that adversely impacts their capacity to strong a mortgage. Further, concentrating this sensitive statistics indoors 3 groups generates an entire lot of publicity. The September 2017 Equifax breach located out the credit score records of approximately 150M Americans. Alternative lending the use of blockchain technology gives a much less expensive, more green, and extra stable approach of creating personal loans available to a larger pool of customers. With a cryptographically secure, decentralized take a look at in of in advance bills, users could in all likelihood request loans based totally on a global credit score score rating. A lot of organizations are on foot in this area. Dharma Labs, as an example, is a device for tokenized debt. It seeks to offer builders the gear and requirements vital for setting up on line debt markets.

Meanwhile, Bloom intends to bring credit score score scoring to blockchain and is designing a protocol for coping with the identity, threat, and credit rating score the use of blockchain era. Another opportunity to conventional loans is P2P lending. Individuals and organizations may also additionally loan to and borrow from each other while now not having to cope with the stringent policies of banks. These loans frequently take region on fintech systems. The groups that administer the ones systems do chance assessments, be given applications, and preserve lenders' coins and collections from debtors in escrow fee range. While such operations enhance financing, in addition they convert fintech organizations into intermediaries. But there's a restrained area for 1/3 activities in Defi (decentralized finance) lending, wherein smart contracts put off the want for a relied on intermediary. Defi lending gives actual P2P finance – creditors and debtors deal without delay with each specific at their personal danger the usage of bitcoin. As of January 2022, the general charge locked in Defi changed into $ninety two.36B, up from $34.69B the preceding one year. For Defi lending, borrowers want to placed up collateral by using using using depositing, via a smart agreement, a sum in a distant places cash that is as a minimum similar to the quantity they want to borrow. To hedge in competition to the fee swings of bitcoin, numerous lending swimming swimming pools ask borrowers to overcollateralize their loans. The disadvantage for debtors is that hobby expenses have a tendency to be higher in Defi loans than in traditional finance, usually exceeding 10 in line with cent. On the alternative aspect, the temptation is that the price of the foreign exchange borrowed can skyrocket, due to this they may generate a handsome earnings.

BankSocial is an Ethereum-based totally platform that ensures to be the primary blockchain-based totally absolutely P2P lending network. It employs a social consensus lending pool and compensates its humans to maintain tokens used for financing loans. Members stake tokens in go back for the part of the interest received from every loan. Lendo makes a comparable claim but in a unique play. It concentrates on microloans, eschews collaterals, and includes a market for buying and selling default money owed. It accumulates a element of each mortgage in a reimbursement fund, and that fraction is straight away provided to the lender within the case of default to offset the loss. That said, there's a manner for installation, regulated institutions to slither into the Defi area while now not having to increase their risk urge for food. Lending platform Aave, for instance, has advanced a permissioned liquidity pool that allows nice "whitelisted" institutions — folks who bypass due diligence necessities — to lend and borrow cryptocurrency.

Insurance

The majority of modern insurance blockchain programs are geared at increasing operational effectiveness. Insurance corporations are using blockchain to preserve prices, boost up marketplace get admission to, and improve purchaser studies in choice to building new products.

It is feasible to lessen insurance organization processing times and prices with the useful resource of the use of a blockchain to provide a single deliver of reality for transactions amongst events.

Because of the immutability and version control of blockchain era, many insurance blockchain tasks encompass worldwide collaborations or transactions.

Blockchain-based definitely truely maritime coverage platform Insurwave is the cease give up end result of a partnership among EY and blockchain startup Guardtime. For superior risk checks and quicker claims payments, the Insurwave device uses Corda's disbursed ledger technology to construct an immutable database among shippers and insurers.

According to PwC, the reinsurance agency, which gives coverage to insurers, stands to preserve as a whole lot as $10 billion with the aid of the use of blockchain. Blockchain may be used to decorate risk analytics, automate operations, and expedite the charge of claims.

Contracts may be created and controlled on distributed ledgers with the assist of B3i Re. The ledger maintains tune of any changes to settlement phrases, making it much less difficult for activities to barter and making sure settlement clarity always. Manual processing is liable to forgery, this is removed the use of a allocated ledger.

Here, clients may moreover have a have a look at more about 12 insurance blockchain experiments. We've also checked out how blockchain could probable effect the insurance corporation in-depth.

Charity

For individuals who donate to charity reasons, blockchain allows you to hint exactly in which your cash have become going when it arrived and who received it.

As a result, blockchain may also furthermore help resolve the longstanding issues about charity objects, which consist of the organisational inefficiencies (or even monetary wrongdoing) that would prevent coins from accomplishing the humans it is supposed for.

The BitGive Foundation, a Bitcoin-primarily based definitely charity, makes use of a regular and transparent allotted ledger to allow individuals better perception into the receipt and usage of rate variety.

It has moreover added GiveTrack, a blockchain-based totally multidimensional contribution platform that permits for the transmission, monitoring and recording of philanthropic cash transactions in the route of the place. Charities may additionally additionally gather self warranty with participants by the usage of way of the use of GiveTrack.

Travel & mobility

Chapter 3: Automotive manufacturing

For example, the usage of a blockchain to reveal the possession of real gadgets, such as automobile additives, is a extremely good use case for the era. Unlike centralized databases, that are prone to hacking, human errors, and manipulation, blockchains can't be altered and are not managed through the use of a single birthday celebration. Blockchain generation could probably perceive and get rid of counterfeit additives from the supply chain. The generation may even significantly impact automobile recollects, which are anticipated to have an effect on round 32 million vehicles by the use of 2020. Blockchain generation recollects can be tailored to precise automobiles primarily based on the area of the components. MOBI is a vehicle and element monitoring software program that Ford, BMW, Honda, and GM have labored on for a while (Mobility Open Blockchain Initiative). The Vehicle Identity (VID) Standard creates "begin certificates" for cars inside the form of virtual ledgers that maintain their protection statistics and allow for pass-border registration. As some different instance, Ocean Protocol and Daimler have teamed up with the decentralized facts change to look at how blockchain might be used to percentage deliver chain statistics across Daimler's commercial enterprise hubs and partners. GM and BMW have additionally joined with MOBI to alternate self-driving vehicle records the use of blockchain technology.

Car leasing & income

Blockchain generation has the functionality to streamline the leasing, buying, and selling of automobiles, this is now a bulky way for all occasions concerned.

With blockchain era, Visa teamed with transaction manage enterprise DocuSign in 2015 to simplify car leasing.

Leasing an vehicle using the Visa-DocuSign device is possible, and the transaction is recorded on the blockchain. A leasing agreement and coverage policy are signed from the motive pressure's seat, and the blockchain is updated with that records.

Companies like Estonia-based totally carVertical are the use of blockchain technology to higher display screen the statistics of used vehicles for customers who want to buy them. In a unmarried ledger, carVertical tracks data from diverse assets, collectively with leasing and coverage statistics, on motors. A more entire document on a vehicle's facts is then generated using the ledger data, and the VINs entered by the use of customers.

Ride-hailing

In comparison to decentralisation, adventure-hailing apps like Uber and Lyft function as dispatching centres and lease algorithms to alter motive force fleets (and dictate what they price). With a allocated ledger, drivers and passengers may also construct a extra man or woman-driven, fee-oriented economic device. Blockchain can also exchange that dynamic.

Arcade City, as an instance, uses a blockchain to streamline all transactions. Unlike distinct enjoy-hailing offerings, this one lets in drivers to select out their charges (in exchange for a part of passenger prices), and the blockchain information every transaction.

Because of this, Arcade City can attraction to professional drivers who pick out out to run their very very own transportation groups in choice to be dominated via enterprise headquarters. For instance, drivers can also installation their consumer base and offer unique offerings like transport or roadside assist in this case with the aid of offering greater services. Arcade City stated in January 2021 that it'd make its code open-source to allow for added peer-to-peer transactions in the gaming employer.

Drive is every different blockchain-based experience-sharing software program application. The agency is now based totally genuinely in Bangalore however plans to increase to extremely good Indian cities . The app uses a "custom designed smart contracts" device amongst drivers and passengers, in which drivers stake Drife's DRF token to be decided on for trips. To use the Drive app, drivers pay an annual subscription price.

Public transportation

As cities have grown, so has the burden on many transportation networks, which may be steeply-priced and inefficient. A metropolis's capability to better apprehend how its residents use public transit alternatives might be superior through the usage of blockchain era. Dovu is an tremendous example of a blockchain-sponsored software program that allows commuters to proportion their journey and transit data, such as how they utilise public transportation and motorbike-sharing, after so that you can pay them with crypto tokens. Go-Ahead, a mass transportation business employer, has furthermore collaborated with the companies usage of blockchain era may likely bring about a extra inexperienced and simplified approach. There are many techniques to utilise a public ledger, as an instance, to hold and trade information on vehicle performance or on-time regular overall performance.

Trucking

It's no longer best virtual transactions that may be tracked and documented the usage of blockchain; actual goods like freight vehicles also may be. On the alternative hand, private blockchain networks have benefits over public ones.

The Blockchain in Transportation Alliance (BiTA) become created to set enterprise standards and teach its participants. Approximately 500 individuals on this commercial blockchain affiliation are working to installation the frameworks so that you can alter how the trucking and transportation sectors perform.

In addition to enhancing transactions, transport monitoring, and fleet management, blockchain may additionally assist fantastic assets and growth fleet performance. For instance, following a vehicle that assets materials and recording whether or no longer or no longer appropriate storage situations have been maintained within the path of any delays can also help with food contamination tracking. The matching of drivers and gadgets to be added with vehicles in a particular vicinity may additionally moreover assist optimise routes.

This quarter, however, dreams the cooperation of all events worried: small and huge companies, final-mile shippers, and massive transportation businesses. In the absence of complete buy-in, the system will no longer absolutely optimise.

Air journey

Consider all of the data needed to ebook a flight: names, begin dates, credit card numbers, passport numbers, very last places, and, relying at the technique used, hotel or apartment automobile statistics. With blockchain generation, guests may moreover have a more stable revel in and one that is more available for them. The addition of a virtual token to a bodily charge price ticket will increase safety. When a smart settlement is covered within the price ticket token, airlines can better display and control the sale and utilization of tickets. Other uses encompass growing more correct protection statistics, retaining off overbooking, and additional. Russia's S7

Airlines has advanced a personal, Ethereum-based totally completely blockchain to reduce the time it takes to pay its shops from 14 days to 15 seconds. The airline said in 2019 that it had dealt with $1 million in month-to-month charge rate tag income on its blockchain. In distinct phrases, in 2019. Decentralized travel marketplaces like Winding Tree's are getting rid of the need for intermediaries. Employees of a prime enterprise may additionally buy amusement excursion tickets on American Airlines' market at a company charge with out going through a adventure control organisation.

The airline loyalty programme is every one-of-a-kind location where blockchain has already been used. As part of the Kris+ manner of lifestyles app from Singapore Airlines, a blockchain-primarily based absolutely digital pockets converts miles to bitcoin, that might then be redeemed at participating service provider places. Flyers who enrol on this programme get factors for destiny flights, but they can also use the ones factors to make quite a number different purchases, in conjunction with motel stays and automobile leases. Many of these issues can be solved with the beneficial aid of blockchain, which incorporates the ones related to aviation maintenance and restore (MRO). Because of prolonged overall performance, PwC believes that blockchain may additionally moreover reduce MRO prices with the beneficial useful resource of spherical $three.5 billion. Delays, costs, and errors are related to manually tracking and tracking spare aeroplane additives. An aircraft's configuration and safety facts can be correctly documented the usage of blockchain, which makes use of digital statistics. This information can be blanketed into algorithms to help with predictive safety and decrease downtime. Additionally, it can be used to music down providers and components brief and lift the resale fee of plane in the future.

Aerospace & protection

According to Accenture, sixty one% of aerospace and military corporations paintings with blockchain or allocated ledger technology. Parts inventory and verification and worker certification tracking can be made extra available with blockchain technology.

One such marketplace is GoDirect Trade (a subsidiary of Honeywell Aircraft), which utilises blockchain to put it up for sale aerospace additives available on the market. Each of its 25,000 quantities has a record inside the ledger detailing while it modified into serviced and manufactured. This information is then utilised to fast listing reconditioned additives by using FAA guidelines, decreasing out the time-ingesting manual and paperwork-massive strategies which have traditionally characterised the aerospace additives reselling organization.

A new production net web site for Thales Group's naval shipbuilding company in France has established a blockchain device to ensure that the potential's shipbuilding tool meets the standards of NATO.

Blockchain is likewise being utilized by worldwide places like the United States and Russia. Russia's Ministry of Defense released a blockchain studies lab in 2018. As of this 365 days, america Department of Defense has partnered with the blockchain organization SIMBA Chain to create a gadget for securely moving and tracking studies and development information.

Hospitality

Commissions paid to 1/3-birthday party reserving organizations fee massive lodge chains as much as 30 constant with cent of their entire profits. Between 18 and 22 steady with cent of the profits of small chains and unbiased hotels is spent on 1/three-birthday party offerings.

Hoteliers can also maintain a more huge part of income because of blockchain generation's overall performance within the reserving and selling system.

A B2B excursion market like Winding Tree has been jogging with hotels, airways, and tourist bureaus to broaden a decentralised B2B tour marketplace. When hotels make their API available to on-line excursion agencies, it's far referred to as "positioned up or perish" (OTAs). For the OTA to start promoting the motel inventory at once, the 2 businesses can conduct direct transactions.

Chapter 4: Infrastructure & energy

Industrial IoT

One of the most promising programs of blockchain era is the capability for any tool to securely connect with distinct devices and conduct transactions without the need for any centralised manipulate or authority the least bit. One of the benefits of blockchains is that they'll be used to preserve facts from a huge huge fashion of devices, getting rid of the want for an intermediary among them. Software updates, bugs, and energy manage could all be treated through the usage of gadgets talking with each other on their very very own. Hyundai Merchant Marine (HMM), a logistics business enterprise in South Korea, examined a blockchain device created with Samsung SDS in 2017 that used IoT sensors for real-time monitoring of shipment. Ship arrival and departure, payments of lading, and cargo tracking were all dealt with through the "paperless operation."Blockchain networks for Internet of Things (IoT) devices in internet infrastructure and smart metropolis transportation have just been constructed via Helium and NetObjex, respectively. Others are addressing IoT network security. Connected sensors in vital infrastructure collectively with energy flora and transportation have sparked privateness and protection problems. To make certain the integrity of business device networks, groups like Xage are relying on blockchain's tamper-evidence ledgers.

3-D printing

A mouse click on is all it takes to deliver the virtual statistics wished in 3-D printing and "additive manufacturing" (aka constructing three-d subjects by means of the use of including layer-upon-layer material). Communicating and monitoring devices is now easier, ensuing in greater green virtual supply chains.

To help the three-D printing and additive manufacturing industries to growth and scale, blockchain era may be used to support those developing infrastructures and minimise protection dangers, shield highbrow assets from theft, and expedite assignment control.

BASECAMP (Blockchain Approach for Supply Chain Additive Manufacturing Parts) task includes america Air Force and SIMBA Chain. To hold three-d-found components steady and tamper-proof, the blockchain platform registers and video display gadgets them. By imparting traceable and verifiable records of three-d designs, blockchain solutions like MainChain from Victory and GumboNet from Data Gumbo help in making sure the integrity of 3-D printing.

Construction, shape, & constructing

It's a pretty regulated quarter this is primarily based closely on a big fashion of professionals to finish complicated responsibilities. It might be difficult and time-eating to confirm their legitimacy, paintings high-quality, and reliability. General contractors may additionally furthermore locate it much less difficult to authenticate identities and reveal paintings throughout numerous agencies with a blockchain-based surroundings.

While smart contracts also can make it much less hard to deliver well timed payments tied to venture milestones mechanically, blockchain generation can also assist confirm that constructing elements are procured from the right belongings and are of right terrific.

With using a blockchain, the Amsterdam-based totally production business enterprise HerenBouw may moreover need to record all of the orders and payments made during a massive improvement task within the city.

Real belongings

Real property transactions are complex via a loss of openness before, in the course of, and after the sale. Public documents can also in all likelihood include inaccuracies or fraud. It is feasible to dispose of the need for paper records and boost up transactions the usage of blockchain technology. This improves the efficiency of all events taking part within the transaction and reduces transaction prices. Helps to affirm all papers are accurate and verifiable through the use of the use of real belongings blockchain era to screen and switch land titles. Propy's blockchain-primarily based clever agreement generation targets to offer safe residence purchases. Deeds, contracts, and one of a kind criminal files are recorded digitally on the blockchain and in hard replica. For finance, name, and mortgage industries, Ubitquity offers a SaaS blockchain platform. Tokenized assets titles are being created the use of blockchain generation in partnership with Stewart Title of Washington, D.C., among unique clients.

Blockchain can probably permit the acquisition of digital land at the same time as used alongside aspect virtual truth and video video video video games. Individuals and corporations have spent file quantities for virtual actual property at the Decentraland metaverse recreation platform. For $2.Four million simply really worth of cryptocurrencies in November 2020, the Metaverse Group purchased 116 assets plots on The Sandbox metaverse, at the identical time as a person paid $450,000 to stay round the corner to rapper Snoop Dogg.

Energy management

Another enterprise, energy manage, has been mainly centralized within the past. Either deal with a reseller who buys from a large electric powered enterprise corporation like Duke Energy or National Grid in case you're in the US or UK, or drift through an established energy preserving corporation.

Distributed ledgers can probably lessen (or eliminate) the want for intermediaries, clearly as they have in exclusive sectors. Firms like LO3 Energy are reexamining traditional techniques of replacing electricity.

On the Energy Web Chain platform, LO3 Energy's Pando product lets software customers engage in "decentralized strength producing schemes," allowing customers to create, buy, and sell energy.

Other agencies have employed blockchain to offer green energy get right of entry to. Acciona Energy and Iberdrola,massive Spanish electricity companies, are utilizing blockchain to confirm the renewable strength it generates by using using using tracking its assets.

Waste manage

To decrease landfill trash, recycling is one of the maximum splendid strategies to do it. However, recycling may be a difficult and time-eating approach that is not commonly fascinating. Current recycling structures could probably benefit from optimization the use of a blockchain-primarily based method. There is a slew of new businesses bobbing up to sell recycling. Used plastic can be exchanged for cash or virtual tokens at The Plastic Bank, taking element with IBM to make its recycling solution available worldwide. Communities can also additionally use W2V Eco Solutions to provide coins to residents who kind their recycling effectively. Blockchain-primarily based software software from RecycleGO permits recycling companies display and enhance their nearby deliver chain more correctly. More set up groups like BASF have joined the marketing marketing campaign. This is further to IBM. Keychain, a blockchain-based totally really plastic recycling trial, may be launched with the useful resource of BASF in August 2020. Using first-rate "chemical barcode tags," plastic makers can higher screen their products throughout their lifespan and encourage recycling because of this take a look at. In addition to NOVA Chemicals and Deloitte, the partnership consists of Save-On-Food.

Oil & fuel

The potential of blockchain to automate the validity and enforcement of contracts amongst severa activities within the supply chain is one of the primary benefits of the oil and fuel area.

The Abu Dhabi National Oil Company, for instance, employs a blockchain-primarily based truly tool to display screen production volumes accurately and automatically and to carry out transactions at severa stages of oil and gas manufacturing, from the manufacturing side to the consumer issue. For both time and transparency, this minimizes the time it takes to execute a transaction.

Chapter 5: Healthcare

Health records exchanges

Aloss of functionality to soundly switch facts across systems is a super trouble for healthcare companies. Improved evaluation, remedy, and monetary universal performance may also additionally end stop end result from changing affected man or woman facts among clinical experts. Using blockchain technology, healthcare organizations, payers, and one in all a kind stakeholders may exchange network get proper of access to with out compromising the integrity or safety of affected person facts. For instance, HealthVerity participates in this marketplace, the usage of blockchain generation to address access and permissions for health facts exchanges. Others are leveraging blockchain technology to enhance issuer statistics manage. Aetna, Cognizant, Humana, MultiPlan, Quest Diagnostics, UnitedHealth Group, and others have joined Synaptic Health Alliance to make certain that their provider directories are up to date. Because the facts is saved and up to date in a favored, available database, those corporations can also moreover keep time thru manner of replacing this statistics with one more. A medical doctor's ability to workout in certain states can be showed thru a blockchain-based totally definitely credential verification device developed by way of the use of way of Hashed Health.

Vaccine distribution & tracking

As blockchain allows for actual-time perception into the deliver chain, delivering vaccinations at some point of an epidemic is important because it lets in for a speedier reaction to supply interruptions. This superior visibility can also useful resource in identifying any vaccination batches that need to be recalled after an unfavorable event.

Many worldwide locations, like Malaysia and Singapore, have already carried out vaccination certificate that may be traced once more to their actual batch the usage of blockchain technology. As a stop end result of this settlement, residents of the 2 nations can right away verify the validity in their credentials when they travel over their borders.

Genomics

Researchers in the issue of genomics artwork with large datasets regularly housed in cloud-based totally repositories for clean get admission to.

In the case of a records breach, touchy statistics might be at risk because of a single factor of failure in this storage method. As a surrender quit result, lots and lots of humans's genetic data is probably under the authority of a single business enterprise. Scientific evidence is at hazard if political critiques and prison recommendations trade. This is what climate scientists positioned out following the 2016 U.S. Elections.

To fight these troubles, the genomics business enterprise seems to the computing grids applied in Bitcoin mining for concept.

Ethereum-based totally truly Bioinformatics studies using computing and garage nodes in Zenome's system. Nodes inside the machine are paid for his or her offerings with the beneficial aid of the clients. In addition, Zenome aspires to defend the privacy and manage of clients' genetic information. Pharmaceutical businesses, as an instance, can also additionally buy get entry to to character facts on a brief or everlasting foundation from users who have uploaded it to the blockchain.

People also can placed up their raw DNA facts files to EncrypGen, which eliminates all in my opinion identifiable facts and sensitive statistics. The Gene-Chain market offers quite a few cash for the sale of those documents. DNA is EncrypGen's cryptocurrency coin.

Nebula Genomics offered the primary genomic NFT at auction in May 2021. The NFT aesthetically and artistically portrayed the primary direct genomic sequencing technique by way of Professor George Church in 1984. The look at group emphasised that the genome is a non-fungible illustration of important, non-public information for all people.

Despite its unconventional nature, this initiative gives numerous sensible blessings. Using Church's genomic NFT, Oasis Labs has decoded the right area of his whole genome's digital statistics, that is saved on Oasis Network. It moreover consists of Oasis Labs' Parcel, a privacy-keeping records governance SDK that works with the blockchain.

Claims manage

Health care's decrease decrease back cease is gradual, convoluted, and steeply-priced. Some of those strategies is probably expedited and costs decreased if blockchain is used on the facet of statistics standards. For instance, in claims control, severa intermediaries attention on standardizing information due to the complex and changeable approaches involved. Payers should gather a significant style of information from many assets to set up the offerings a affected individual has received and the precise plan below which the affected person is blanketed. Doctors can not execute their jobs efficiently inside the event that they don't know how a bargain to charge their sufferers. Everyone desires to realise where a claim presently stands in its lifetime. For example, a system known as the Intelligent Healthcare Network superior with the useful resource of Change Healthcare tracks each of the sports stated above at some degree within the claim's lifespan (information submitted for evaluate, the evaluate itself, approval or denial, and plenty of others.) Many public blockchain tasks have slowed transaction processing pace and scalability. Five hundred fifty transactions steady with second are the commonplace for Change Healthcare, which claims to help as plenty as 50 million transactions each day at the community.

Pharma

As a pharmaceutical enterprise organisation, it isn't always identified as rapid-paced. Despite the business enterprise's recognition on innovation and hassle answers, medical trying out, FDA clearances, and different strategies are pressured with the aid of a large quantity of crimson tape.

Faster innovation, extra regulation of manufacturing, and in addition progressive clinical statistics safety are all possible with a blockchain ledger.

Blockchain technology may additionally additionally likely be used to make sure the safe manufacture of prescribed drugs. Errors may be identified and the foundation purpose tracked down. As a end result, producers are better capable of forestall recollects or as a minimum communicate with shops greater hastily within the case of a volatile drug alert.

In 2017, Chronicled, in partnership with many primary pharmaceutical companies and supply chain heavyweights, created the MediLedger Network. To validate pharmaceutical returns, the initiative employs a blockchain-based totally completely tracking tool.

Covid-19 counterfeiting is a good sized trouble inside the pharmaceutical agency, it truely is why MediLedger and Deloitte mounted a partnership in July 2020.

Chapter 6: Government & public information

In handling public services, blockchain may moreover moreover assist lessen paper-based totally operations, reducing fraud, and promoting duty between government and the people they serve. Some governments are beginning to see the advantages of blockchain and are taking steps to use it. A proper instance is the Swedish Land Registry, which has looked at using blockchain for land registration to reduce fraud and ownership disputes. Smart contracts have moreover been tested to perform property transactions. States during the us of the united states have in the end brought comparable measures. BitFury, a startup based in Eastern Europe, has teamed with the Georgian authorities to protect and screen authorities statistics.

Voting

Voters' identities must be proven, vote casting want to be tracked, and the winner should be decided the usage of accurate tallies. There can be no need for a recount inside the destiny if blockchain generation may be used to make sure the integrity of the balloting procedure via doing away with voter fraud and notable irregularities.

When votes are recorded as transactions on the blockchain, governments and residents may be certain that no votes were changed or withdrawn or invalid votes have been introduced. Follow My Vote, a blockchain vote casting start-up has publicly made its patent-pending forestall-to-quit blockchain vote casting system available.

Blockchain-based absolutely completely voting is being advanced thru a few other commercial corporation known as Agora. A specialized blockchain document is used to avoid election fraud. In Sierra Leone's 2018 elections, the platform became tested in a confined potential and furnished outcomes much like expert tallies.

Gun tracking

Gun possession and use may additionally revel in the allotted ledger of the blockchain. It might be feasible to trace the origins of illegally acquired weapons if gun possession data had been recorded and connected together the usage of blockchain.No Fly List records may be integrated into blockchain transaction facts to save you illicit weapon transactions in the long run.

Law enforcement

Blockchain era may also moreover help police investigations through supplying a further layer to ensure the integrity of the chain of evidence isn't tampered with in any way. Blockchain might also additionally find out suspicious transaction styles, offering government a heads-up while a person participates in economic behavior that can be considered illegal.

For regulation enforcement, this innovation is coming from startups. Using close to-situation communications chips and a blockchain machine, Chronicled is building tamper-evidence containers that may be sealed and the contents of which can be registered.

Bitcoin registries are being continuously looked for unusual transactions and histories with the useful resource of Elliptic, it definitely is constructing an alarm device that could tell law authorities.

Federal mail

This includes america Postal Service, this is considering the use of blockchain generation to enhance its operations and customer service. USPS may additionally hold money and time via way of the usage of a allotted ledger technology monitoring device that uses dispensed ledgers. According to a 2016 Office of Inspector General assessment, the business corporation may also employ blockchain to optimize its financial offerings (consisting of coins orders), installation a higher "Internet of Postal Things," increase patron identification authentication and expedite deliver chain control. Voters may be despatched "token-connected QR codes," and their signatures can be stored on a blockchain as part of a patent software submitted with the useful aid of the United States Postal Service in August 2020. A service that makes use of blockchain to provide postage labels, CaseMail, became licensed as an NFT within the following 12 months with the useful resource of the employer. The postal issuer may additionally moreover make tracking a package deal's adventure a great deal much less complex by manner of employing digitally stamped labels.

Public assist

Often slowed thru pink tape, blockchain implementation may additionally advantage the general public help tool. When dishing out humanitarian useful resource to refugees, the United Nations World Food Program (WFP) has started using blockchain era. The World Food Program (WFP) uses blockchain and biometric identification generation to offer comfort right away to refugees for the reason that they regularly can not create financial institution money owed.

The World Food Program (WFP) has installed iris scanners at refugee camps in Jordan to pick out out folks that want monetary manual for his or her meals. All transactions are recorded fast on a personal blockchain, and the individual's blockchain-enabled account is right away credited with the fee.

Chapter 7: Retail & CPG

Retail

Faith in the retail business employer is particularly primarily based on clients' receive as real with within the market in which they make their purchases. For instance, Amazon's success with customers is based on consumer agree with. The decentralization of take into account thru blockchain generation would possibly probably make it greater closely tied to the dealers on multiple markets and structures.

Breezy, for example, is a startup imparting decentralized blockchain utilities to hyperlink producers and brands, shops, 1/three-birthday celebration sellers, content material fabric businesses, and customers while now not having an middleman.

Furthermore, Germany-primarily based absolutely Gambio has installed GAMB (Global Alliance of Merchants at the Blockchain), a decentralized marketplace that empowers traders with the aid of providing them entire manage over their retail place. GMB tokens, which provide shops the electricity to vote on market problems, make it viable for any shop to enroll within the alliance.

LVMH, however, has teamed up with Microsoft and ConsenSys, a blockchain commercial enterprise corporation, to establish a platform to certify expensive devices the use of blockchain. It's feasible to tune a product's journey from format thru distribution the use of AURA, the platform. AURA gives a in addition layer of safety in opposition to counterfeit merchandise and fraud for the corporation's popularity.

The metaverse will ultimately have its retail establishments. There are plans for Walmart to create its cryptocurrency and NFTs, and the business organisation is also making plans to open a digital store.

E-alternate

Lower transaction charges and tighter transaction safety may alter e-trade with blockchain era. Retail behemoths Walmart, Amazon, and Alibaba, have all started out looking on the capability of the blockchain as a fee device. In March 2020, Alibaba carried out for a patent in Brazil for a blockchain-based totally clearly transaction system.

Global alternate may want to likely advantage from blockchain considering it'd permit for better traceability, provide proof of transport, and display settlement specifics without fear of records tampering.

The Home Depot has teamed up with IBM to leverage blockchain generation to govern its issuer ties higher. The shop has decreased supplier lawsuits and the time it takes to settle them with the beneficial useful resource of keeping a shared, time-stamped report of the motion of products at some stage in shipping and receiving.

Food & beverage

Whether it became E. Coli, salmonella, or unintended horse meat, the food, and beverage sector has had its honest percentage of mishaps. Manufacturers and providers can be capable of prevent such errors the usage of blockchain era. With blockchain, food contamination can be traced to its supply seeing that it is a decentralized ledger that statistics, saves, and video display gadgets statistics. Food processors, stores, and clients all experience the gadget, which permits them to prevent or lessen recalls; retailers, that could react more hastily and successfully; and customers, who can remember that the meals they purchase is steady to devour. IBM's Food Trust community, which uses a allotted ledger-based at the blockchain, now consists of Walmart and Sam's Club. As early as 2018, merchants started out out inquiring for records from their carriers, specifically people who offer leafy veggies, to be blanketed in a big database via using the subsequent 12 months. Using the generation, food can be traced once more to its supply more , it is a large benefit within the events like tracing the supply of inflamed gadgets. The blockchain might also moreover act as an duty platform to reduce meals remembers, mislabeled goods, and uncertainty about in which a problem passed off, as long as clearly all and sundry involved consents. When a QR Code is scanned, the product's complete course to the customer's basket may be seen the use of blockchain-based totally honestly monitoring. Nestlé and Carrefour are putting a similar provider to the take a look at with purchasers in France for its Mousline mashed potatoes, constructing on their 2018 blockchain check with IBM Food Trust. By scanning the QR code at the package of Mousline, consumers can trace the product's journey from farmer to Nestle plant to their nearby Carrefour preserve.

Cannabis

The legalization of marijuana in Canada and the growing momentum for legalization inside the United States have resulted in huge costs on generation and research for the hashish enterprise.

A apparent and stable gadget for tracking manufacturing and distribution is probably fine inside the legalized cannabis employer, that is expected to be carefully regulated. The functionality to tune merchandise from farm to dispensary with the help of blockchain technology may moreover want to enhance product protection and regulatory compliance.

With Chain.Io, Mile High Labs, a dealer and producer of CBD merchandise have created a deliver chain that can be tracked using the blockchain. It does not in truth deliver chains that Mile High Labs is inquisitive about the usage of blockchain era for.

In addition, IBM has recommended that governments use blockchain generation to expose the origins and distribution of marijuana.

Gift card & loyalty applications

A present card and loyalty software program software machine may be made greater rate-effective and solid through the usage of manner of using blockchain generation because of the fact fewer intermediaries are required to conduct the difficulty of playing cards and income transactions.

As a cease result of blockchain's precise verification capacity, fraud safety degrees may be raised, saving cash and preventing unauthorized clients from gaining access to stolen accounts.

For example, Loyyal is leveraging blockchain to guide and confirm the price of loyalty awards just so they may be exchanged at some stage in multiple sectors (think about multi-branded "Airline/Retailer/Consumer" rewards).

Agriculture & herbal assets

Crops & agriculture

For agriculture, blockchain has the functionality to revolutionize the arena past the protection and traceability troubles highlighted in the context of meals and beverage. A decentralized blockchain machine could probably help the rural supply chain via the usage of improving transactions, growing the marketplace, and customizing logistics for individual products. It is possible to create self belief amongst consumers which have in no manner met earlier than through a blockchain file. Helps the marketplace boom, encouraging more healthful opposition amongst companies. AgriDigital is already using blockchain technology to digitize the purchase, sale, and storage of grain, and it dreams to make bigger to specific commodities hastily. For farmers to stock customers, it centralizes and secures the control in their connections with each other.

Additionally, blockchain may also provide new income resources for farmers, permitting them to make extra cash. The CO_2 Offset Market, for instance, encourages the growth of hemp, a carbon-bad crop. A tokenizing crop is a feasible option for farmers who need to resell their carbon credits.

Animal husbandry

Animal husbandry, like agriculture, benefits from blockchain era to boom food safety, traceability, and sustainability. An animal's genome, feed, and scientific facts may also moreover all be related together inside the form of an animal's information the use of the blockchain era advanced with the aid of way of food safety startup Neogen in collaboration with the meals-targeted blockchain platform Ripe Technology. It's a "record of agree with for cattle from begin via to the patron," says NSF Verify, which employs blockchain generation. Animals are implanted with radio-frequency identity (RFID) tags at delivery. Their movements are tracked and recorded on a blockchain using the platform built thru the usage of NSF International and one among a type industry experts. Breeder, a British startup, gives a cell phone app for tracking and storing facts approximately cows. Using Breeder's blockchain era, farmers can song the overall overall performance and development of individual animals, permitting them to make higher rearing alternatives and lowering the time it takes to deliver an animal to marketplace. Regarding environmental obligation, BASF and arc-net,chemical manufacturers, teamed together in 2018 "to assist animal manufacturing fee chain." Meat, milk, and egg products may additionally moreover now be traced the use of arc-blockchain net generation and BASF's AgBalance Livestock sustainability calculation tool.

Fishing

Approximately 20% to 30% of the fish market within the United States is illegally harvested. According to the Wall Street Journal, fishing is one of the maximum exploitative industries inside the international regarding using slave hard work. Blockchain-based era could in all likelihood help the sector grow to be more sustainable, environmentally great, and legally compliant. By registering net types and quantities on a blockchain, it is possible to display if fishing boats go lower returned to port with the large sort of nets they departed with. It is possible to make use of the blockchain to select out and music character fish. When setting up a blockchain-based definitely completely system for verifying in which, at the same time as, and the manner fish have been accrued, the World Wildlife Fund joined with ConsenSys and SeaQuest Fiji. Scan the QR code together with your cellular telephone to confirm that you're looking for jail, sustainable tuna that wasn't caught using slave exertions or below abusive walking occasions

Logging & timber

As said with the aid of the Endowment for Forestry and Communities within the United States, blockchain generation may also assist defend the global deliver chain of lumber. By the stop of 2020, the ForesTrust Blockchain Network is probably able to "music wooden and wood fiber from the wooded area to the patron." The mission hobbies to promote customer consider in the global wooden trade through making it much less difficult to trace the origins of the wood imported "blockchain-based carbon credit score and natural capital marketplace" is part of Veridium Labs' plan to lessen carbon emissions. Companies can also additionally acquire and sell carbon credits more hastily and freely, way to the tokenization of carbon credit score rating.

Mining

The mining corporation, which relies on coordinating and taking part with many intermediaries, may want to probably gain considerably from blockchain technology. Consequently, the area has struggled to deal with concerns like fraud and threatening running conditions due to a loss of openness in data. The ability to have a look at the movement of metals and minerals from the mine to the producer might be made more reachable with the usage of blockchain generation.

Chapter 8: Information & conversation

Telecommunications

Telecoms are nicely-located to provide identity control services. For example, cellular corporations music how a good deal statistics customers use every month, how plenty video content material cloth they view every week, what cellular cellphone version humans use, and so on. In unique locations, users take into account their information more than they bear in mind Facebook, Google, or Apple, in line with a ballotvia Analysys Mason. As with non-public facts manipulate, telcos may additionally additionally use their characteristic to provide blockchain-based totally completely identity control offerings. Using a tamper-evidence approach like an get proper of access to token, consumers have to decide whether or no longer they want their records shared with unique agencies. The consumer can be compensated or given a discount at the agency's services in go back for the information they provide. In this case, the blockchain could record all facts accesses. To acquire the blessings of the 5G technology, vendors need to first make investments within the infrastructure as a way to allow them to accomplish that. Co-constructing 5G infrastructure or implementing sharing models for leasing networks can be greater really managed thru openness and immutability of blockchain facts. To take care of beneficial useful resource bidding, brokering, leasing, provider assessment, and settlement agreement, China Unicom and China Telecom have determined to cooperate to gather 5G networks primarily based on a decentralized, blockchain-based totally infrastructure. In terms of infrastructure funding economic savings, it's far predicted that this plan can also keep each corporations $forty five.Five billion. Blockchain technology also can therefore boost organizations' bottom lines.

Additionally, telcos can also rent smart contracts to streamline the negotiation and execution of company-degree agreements (SLAs) at some stage in several worldwide places. This is a time-consuming approach due to the big type of rules, network necessities, and agreement conditions that might exist inside the direction of international locations and provider vendors.

Messaging apps

Cryptocurrency and blockchain generation is being protected into numerous messaging applications.

According to Status, it is a "privacy-first messaging platform." As a end result, "surveilling 1/three events" aren't critical with the open-deliver platform.

Cryptocurrency payments are being considered by means of using manner of Signal, a well-known encrypted messaging provider.

The regulatory context in which these programs perform is hazy at first-rate.

After raising $1.7 billion from personal consumers, Telegram canceled its deliberate $1.2 billion preliminary coin presenting (ICO). This blockchain-based totally TON take a look at patron have become launched around a 12 months later (Telegram Open Network). However, in May 2020, Telegram said that the assignment is probably discontinued due to unresolved SEC talks.

Publishing

There is a slew of potential makes use of for blockchain in publishing, beginning from pirate prevention to rights control. A few publishers dominate the industrial organisation, making it tough for up-and-coming authors to get into it. Authors, editors, translators, and publishers are all reaping the benefits of latest systems that diploma the gambling area for authors and encourage cooperation some of the numerous sports. Ethereum-based totally absolutely publishing platform Bookchin is the brainchild of Montreal-based definitely industrial organization Scenaraex. Each ebook has its smart settlement that determines how and at what rate readers might also additionally get right of access to it. Authors may additionally moreover evade 1/three-party corporations and deal right now with customers at the platform, permitting them to maintain track of exactly wherein each in their e-books is at any given 2d in time. Once a e-book is offered, its rights belong to the purchaser by myself. With smart contracts, Publica hopes to crowdsource the investment of books. A "e-book ICO," as Publica puts it, is a way for writers to elevate cash for his or her projects earlier than they ever begin. By maintaining tokens, readers may also additionally get right of access to a completed e-book posted on the agency's blockchain community. Blockchain technology is wanted to make certain the accuracy of facts critiques and to hint their provenance. Contextual information is probably saved at the blockchain to prevent the manipulation or sharing of data photographs out of context through The New York Times (NYTNews)'s Provenance Project. As part of the Content Authenticity Initiative, the New York Times is likewise partnering with Adobe and Twitter to maintain track of the enhancing records of statistics articles. If the community validates a transaction, it's miles brought to the "blocks" of information that make up the general public blockchain and can not be deleted. Because every block includes the virtual signature of the block in advance than it and contributes to the lock that follows, deleting a block breaks the chain. 2018 proved that this trait, known as censorship-resistance, end up correct even as an open letter grow to be circulated on-line in China alleging sexual harassment at Peking University. It emerge as taken down from WeChat, China's most famous app, and numerous one-of-a-kind internet websites and structures by using the usage of the government. This unnamed character spoke back with the aid of posting the letter on Ethereum's Blockchain – wherein it's going to live all the time. Although the transaction is essentially symbolic, the message is probably hard to locate tillits hex code or transaction ID. To be easy: Governments are free to restrict the block explorers used to experiment a blockchain, as China did regarding the activist pupil's letter. However, public blockchains have because of the truth been outlawed and will as an alternative be utilized by strict prison tips and standards in the country in which they are being used.

corporation in 2020. The corporation uses blockchain generation to offer and validate digital credentials.

Libraries

The Institute of Museum and Library Services provided a $a hundred,000 provide to San José State University's School of Information in December 2017 to assist 12 months-lengthy studies investigating the capability of blockchain technology for records services. It has been speculated that blockchain generation is probably used to growth library offerings through the usage of growing an upgraded metadata repository, inventing a protocol to permit network-primarily based collections, and permitting greater effective rights control for virtual materialsSandra Hirsh and Susan Alman from San Jose State University had been commemorated through using the American Library Association's Center for the Future of Libraries. Case research on how blockchain impacts libraries and what might be completed in the future had been part of a ebook initiative with the ALA. The ebook end up released in November 2019.

Entertainment

Music/amusement rights & IP

Blockchain generation is being used to make content material sharing greater equitable for content cloth manufacturers thru leveraging smart contracts, in which the cash on profits of progressive artwork may be robotically allotted consistent with pre-decided license agreements.

An unbiased track streaming service, Muzika, has joined with cryptocurrency alternate Binance to allow musicians generate coins from their lovers. Muzika has made it easy that it intends to go back ninety% of the profits generated by means of the usage of its artists.

Blockchain startup Mediachain had been constructing a "decentralized media library" until Spotify supplied it in 2017 to understand better track rights holders on Spotify's platform for royalty bills.

JAAK, a blockchain corporation in the United Kingdom, desires to cooperate with song rights holders and different entertainment business enterprise gamers. One of JAAK's initiatives is growing a platform that allows media owners to create "smart content material fabric material" that could self-execute licensing transactions on the Ethereum blockchain the use of their cutting-edge fabric, metadata, and rights repository.

Video streaming

Using blockchain technology to decentralize video encoding, storage, and transport, it's miles viable to reduce video internet site online visitors costs significantly. Netflix, YouTube, and the complete video-distribution agency might be affected.

As quickly as feasible, the VideoCoin Network will begin releasing this capital. Decentralized networks offer cloud video infrastructure (encoding, storage, and transport) as an algorithmic marketplace.

VideoCoins are used to pay for those services on a modern-day blockchain.

On the Ethereum blockchain, Livepeer is every other decentralized network that we have to clients broadcast live movement photographs. Transcoding video for Livepeer Tokens is an opportunity for clients.

Gaming

Online gaming is grow to be a competitive exercise, with coveted titles to be obtained, sizable monetary rewards, or maybe a black market for folks who do not want to compete. For gamers, blockchain generation offers a greater diploma playing trouble in terms of competition and rewards. With the help of the blockchain, it is possible to change tokens while not having a third-party broker. Thanks to a blockchain's dispensed ledger, you may employ the identical characters and skills throughout numerous digital worlds. So they will be capable of earn and switch factors more rapid and resultseasily thru a decentralized community. These changes have already furnished themselves. Founded in 2014, the Huntercoin project was a gaming surroundings wherein gamers were rewarded with in-residence cryptocurrency tokens for their participation (in this situation, HUC coin). Up until 2020, there existed a cryptocurrency referred to as UnikoinGold that have become used for eSports and sports activities making a bet. This cryptocurrency come to be phased out thanks to prison rules. Ethereum-based completely cryptocurrency Enjin Coin backs over one thousand million virtual property in video games that may be exchanged and bought amongst gamers. Platforms for gaming may also additionally moreover provide more consistent and apparent cash transactions with a decentralized blockchain basis. The play-to-earn paradigm can be masses more a success due to NFTs and the metaverse. When Axie Infinity have grow to be famous in 2021, income went from approximately $20K at the start of the 365 days to $246.32M in November. Tokens earned in the sport can be applied in-game or exchanged for real cash on a crypto marketplace. Similar NFT-pushed gameplay has made Blankos Block Party successful, permitting clients to shop for digital vinyl toy figures and layout games. Mythical Games, the economic organization agency inside the lower back of the sport, secured $75 million to assist deliver it and its platform to market through the usage of the middle of 2021. Users' houses can be walked about and explored in Decentraland's digital environment. They might also furthermore pay to join groups, play video video games, take part in place missions, and experience different sports activities that the sector's creators have dreamed up. On this platform in 2022, an Australian Open virtual fact tennis competition will feature a virtual reconstruction of the Rod Laver Arena and virtual meet-americawith expert tennis game enthusiasts.

Social media content

Using blockchain, social media content material carriers have new opportunities to generate cash. Twitter now accepts Bitcoin as a rate technique to inspire customers to help their favourite producers. Meanwhile, TikTok is running with NFT artists to create famous movement photographs. Short video platform Chingari in India now gives an NFT market for its content cloth vendors.

Those that display their aid for up-and-coming artists would probably even achieve the benefits. Decentralized social community BitClout, based definitely in 2021, allows clients to generate their digital distant places money, which they might exchange with specific network individuals for a earnings. It's feasible to speculate on creators the usage of these "author cash"; as an example, in case you trust a particular influencer is probably very a achievement, you may buy their creator cash now and promote them for a far extra price later.

In unique corporations, social media networks are being reimagined as systems in which clients are rewarded for the content they produce and may maintain their anonymity. Incentivizing people to submit right material in return for tokens is one preference.

Sports management

Fans' capability to make investments in the careers of day after brand new sports activities sports stars has historically been restrained to sports activities sports manipulate organizations and massive organizations. However, blockchain era offers the capacity to open up the technique of sponsoring athletes to all lovers. The idea of creating an funding in sportspeople thru the blockchain (and earning rewards) has but to be examined on a big scale. The

Jetcoin Institute, however, has endorsed the notion of fans making an investment of their desired sportsmen with digital cash — in this example, "Jetcoins" — in alternate for a tiny percentage of the athletes' future earnings (further to VIP sports activities, seat improvements, and so on). In cooperation with the Hellas Verona soccer club in Italy, among others, Jetcoin has experimented with this idea.

Gambling

In contemporary years, online gaming has turn out to be extra well-known... However, a number of the maximum crucial issues, which include the great transparency hole, live unresolved to within the meanwhile. Incorporating blockchain era right right into a enterprise agency's operations also can help sell transparency and expand patron self belief. As a end quit result of the generation, truthful video video games may be ensured, as facts on the ledger cannot be modified. Since the device is so decentralized, there may be no need for consider on the identical time as using websites like Wagerr. Through decentralization, on line casinos can preserve their fees in take a look at and make gaming more significantly available to a broader target audience. The capacity to bet anonymously is likewise an essential attention for plenty humans. Filling out pretty a few office work and verifying your identity can also make you a intention for hackers.

Art

Blockchain and tokenization have already been utilized by the art work agency to growth global get right of get entry to to to to the art work marketplace and reduce transaction fees. Art funding blockchain platform Maecenas joined London gallery Dadiani Fine Art in July 2018 to provide fractional ownership in Andy Warhol's "14 Electric Chairs." The public sale changed into accomplished on the Ethereum community using a clever agreement. Another example is Artory, a blockchain-based absolutely organization that gives a public registry for tracking art work records, provenance, and historic records. For its first round of fundraising in April 2019, the agency received $7.Three million from 2020 Ventures and Hasso Plattner Capital. When the artist Beeple makes use of NFTs (not-for-profits tokens) built on blockchain generation, he can track and earn royalties on each piece of art work he sells. In 2021, NFT profits quantity surged from $30 million in Q3'20 to $10.7 billion in Q3'21, a seven-fold increase. This 365 days, the Bored Ape Yacht Club has bought over $1 billion virtually certainly well worth of NFTs, making it the most popular NFT dealer. Celebrity clients, the membership's advantages, and predictions about developing costs and ability resale values sparked most of the hobby. However, like with any disruptive pastime, NFT investment has been debated. More than

$2.2 million of Bored Ape artwork became stolen, on the same time as fantastic YouTubers had their channels bought as NFTs without a permission or information from their proprietors. NFT authentication and protection had been puzzled inside the wake of these instances, raising questions about how valuable a prone asset can be. Critics have mentioned the contradiction of creating an funding in unregulated NFTs on the same time as calling for a centralized platform to help in getting higher stolen artwork.

Chapter 9: Enterprise tech

Cloud computing & garage

For IoT gadgets, cloud offerings need enough processing assets and records garage capacity, that is wasteful. Decentralized cloud offerings enabled by means of blockchain technology have the functionality to improve connection, protection, and compute ability. Salesforce, a organization that gives cloud-based solutions for businesses, has certainly introduced Salesforce Blockchain. In addition to Salesforce's CRM software software utility, the solution adds smart contracts and blockchain-based totally completely clearly information trade to its repertoire. Cloud garage companies generally shop customers' information on a centralized server, which increases the chance of community assaults from hackers. Blockchain cloud garage answers allow garage to be decentralized, decreasing the hazard of attacks which can motive systemic damage and massive information loss. In the terms of 1 reviewer, "Airbnb for report storage" has been coined.

Cryptocurrency task Filecoin goals to incentivize report hosting. Decentralization of Amazon's S3 issuer is probably made possible the usage of this technique. In addition to Union Square Ventures, Naval Ravikant, and the Winklevosses, Protocol Labs has acquired coins from excellent investors. Other token names in garage embody Storj and Siacoin. However, Filecoin is really considered considered one of several projects on this location. Improve protection and decrease transaction expenses with the useful resource of storing records within the cloud using Storj's blockchain-primarily based completely cloud garage machine.

Additionally, customers of Storj have the choice of peer-to-peer renting out their unused virtual garage location, which can also open up a today's market for crowdsourced cloud garage belongings. With blockchain, cloud computing providers also can triumph over the limits of cloud exchanges—networks that allow institutions to hook up with severa clouds, swapping belongings as their processing goals alternate. There is a extra chance of fraud due to the fact a unmarried business enterprise manages cloud exchanges. It is extra difficult for fraudulent transactions and other hacks to take gain of the decentralized nature of cloud exchanges powered with the resource of blockchain era. Since many individuals and companies can also contribute their pc power, the marketplace is stimulated, and costs are stored diploma. This market for laptop assets emerge as set up on Ethereum's disbursed ledger. Tokens referred to as LLC may be used on the iExec market to hire computer belongings, blockchain programs, and datasets.

Internet identity & DNS

For apps you use, your personal data is held on business organisation servers, which have restrained interoperability in current internet international (even the use of Facebook as a log-in nice receives you to date). In the destiny, structures like Serto (formerly uPort) agree with that your identity may be effortlessly transported over the net. An identity control product from IBM known as IBM Verify Credentials uses blockchain generation. Personal privateness and the verification technique are stepped forward via the use of decentralized systems, which allow honest corporations to hassle patron credentials that customers can ultimately use to verify their identity to awesome agencies.

Internet advertising and marketing

As we're privy to it these days, the net turned into built at the backs of improvised advertising and advertising and marketing techniques. The absence of necessities hurts marketers and purchasers due to the reality that advertising and advertising uses quite some mobile bandwidth to load on-line pages. To pay advertisers and clients, Brave's Basic Attention Token (BAT) ICO raised $35 million in plenty much much less than 30 seconds in 2017. Advertisers will listing straight away on Brave's blockchain-based totally definitely browser rather than thru a 3rd-celebration middleman like Google or Facebook. There are fewer however better-focused classified ads for people who pick-in. Additionally, marketers can get right of access to more correct information approximately their spending coins. It's feasible to make coins by using using using selling your personal records on Snovio, a lead-generating internet web site.

Human belongings

Human assets experts face time-eating and hard paintings-vast worrying conditions even as verifying ancient past checks and employment records. Human assets experts may boost up the recruiting tool by way of using the usage of storing employment and criminal facts data in a blockchain ledger, which can't be tampered with. Blockchain-based absolutely Chronobank seeks to revolutionize HR/recruitment by using enhancing quick-time period hiring for in-call for jobs in cleansing and other sectors. Individuals may furthermore discover jobs at the flow into and be paid in bitcoin with out the participation of traditional economic establishments, way to the startup's usage of blockchain technology. When hired, an employee's engagement turns into an vital aspect of humans control, and blockchain may play an essential feature. An wonderful instance is eXo Rewards, a cryptocurrency and blockchain wallet incentive application. Tokens may be exchanged for services and products in a enterprise marketplace, wherein tokens may be exchanged for tokens.

Business & corporate governance

Better accounting practices may also use blockchain's clever settlement and confirmed transaction talents. Smart contracts on Ethereum's public and permissioned blockchains can be managed using the Boardroom app, which offers a governance framework and software software. Organizations can also moreover use the app to check that smart contracts are applied with the aid of the guidelines contained on the blockchain (or to replace the hints themselves). The software application software additionally may be used for shareholder balloting through the usage of proxy and collaborative notion manipulate with the resource of boards of administrators. By "disintermediating the mounted order and manipulate of corporations and other organizational systems," Aragon intends to move an entire lot farther. To help agencies in dealing with their whole global staff using blockchain, Aragon is developing solutions based at the perception that decentralized corporations can address the area's maximum pressing traumatic conditions. When hiring humans and contractors from underdeveloped international locations, the business enterprise believes that blockchain may be a useful tool. Blockchain statistics are incredible for ESG reporting because of their openness and immutability. It is viable to get correct, verifiable, measurable ordinary performance facts, collectively with reducing strength intake or greenhouse gas emissions, via Blockchain and IoT. Data Using Gumbo's GumboNet ESG, this use case is shown. Sensors in the Industrial Internet of Things (IIoT) collect real-time facts on the sports sports of customers, vendors, and logistics company agencies at one cease of the gadget. The information is then in contrast towards sustainability requirements the use of smart contracts. The technology creates and updates auditable and verifiable ESG reviews proper away.

Chapter 10: How To Build Wealth

You may additionally furthermore make rich fast with diverse techniques, from the most modern crypto meme coin to penny inventory trading. Despite their claims of brief cash, scams like those are fraught with danger, and the brilliant majority of members lose all of their cash.

As a forestall cease result, you have to instead consciousness on facts a way to generate cash with the aid of growing an funding technique and adopting an extended-time period mind-set. Get commenced on the path to long-time period monetary safety by using using following those eight smooth steps.

1. Start thru Making a Plan

Financial making plans is step one to being financially stable. Take the time to determine out what you want to obtain, then devise a plan. When it comes to incomes profits, you need a vision and a manner, says Peter Cassciotta, the owner of Asset Management of Lee County. You can also get began for your path to monetary freedom via using hiring a monetary counselor. If you are starting and do not have a good buy money to make investments, an authorized financial planner (CFP) may be the notable preference. It may be extra fee-powerful to keep round for a Robo-advertising and advertising consultant that gives get entry to to financial professionals. Consider making an investment with a Robo-manual like Betterment or Ellevest, which offer controlled portfolios and the capability to talk with advisers.

2. Make a Budget and Stick to It

Even despite the fact that many people despise the letter "b," budgeting is vital to gathering cash. You're more likely to gain executing your technique and amassing your monetary goals if you create a budget and adhere to it. Budgets help you track in which your cash is going every month and assist you keep away from awful habits like overspending that could jeopardize your economic dreams.

3. Build Your Emergency Fund

At Outlook Financial Center, Lori Gross, a financial and investment counselor, explains that credit rating cards go through the brunt of expenses and expenses, which includes immoderate interest expenses. You can also guard your credit score rating and earn hobby on a web economic monetary financial savings account whilst having the safety of information you have got coins set apart for existence's surprising expenses with the useful aid of installing an emergency fund.

four. Automate Your Financial Life

To make certain that you keep in mind to save on your goals or improvement within the course of paying off your debts, automate saving, making an investment, and bill payments. As a cease end result, TBS Retirement Planning president Michael Morgan suggests which you installation automated deductions from your paychecks to cover the whole amount you have deliberate for each of your fees and goals. Saving and making an investment, he explains, areareas wherein that is very beneficial. In this way, you could avoid the need to spend your cash in region of saving it. Once this automatic deduction stops, your donations can be paid on a more ordinary basis," he guarantees.

5. Manage Your Debt

Carrying a debt from month to month isn't an uncommon occurrence. According to an Experian have a examine, the ordinary American owes extra than $90,000 on their credit rating rating gambling playing cards. Mortgages, as an instance, may be seemed as "great" debt because of their low-interest expenses and capacity for wealth boom. Some financial specialists see loan payoffs as a "compelled financial savings account" thinking about you could almost definitely get part of your month-to-month fee at the same time as you sell your home. Every month, rolling over huge quantities of awful debt, which consist of excessive-interest credit score score card bills, would possibly positioned your financial desires at chance. Gross argues it is crucial to have a payback method in place to achieve a debt-free life. Take a have a look at payout strategies just like the snowball or avalanche to see if they may help you get started out out. Paying off debt while although saving coins is viable, and it is also appropriate. So, as your balances decline, you will be able to keep even extra money for emergencies and investments.

6. Max Out Your Retirement Savings

To help you store in your golden years, the federal government offers some of options, all of which financial advisors advocate that you use thoroughly. Making the maximum of your employer's 401(good enough) and character retirement accounts is an notable location to start (IRAs). Consider saving enough to gain your business enterprise's 401(k) in shape in case you can not manage to pay for to make a contribution the criminal most right now. That method that in case your company gives a three% in shape, you will be placing away at least three% of your wages each pay period. No count how little cash you want first of all, do no longer surrender. For the maximum detail, Casciotta provides, her customers installed a piece sum of money and stored it invested over the years. Thus, the pressure of compounding aids in remodeling the ones tiny investments into riches. A purpose-date fund or Robo-manual manages a customized portfolio of price range relying on the huge kind of years you've got left till retirement in case you are not fine a way to begin investing for your 401(okay) or IRA.

7. Stay Diversified

Those who believe the quality manner to get wealthy is to personal vast quantities of Bitcoin also can want to reconsider their mind-set. Investing throughout diverse asset commands may additionally additionally help sturdy your contemporary-day assets at the same time as additionally setting you in a feature to benefit from market downturns. Wells Fargo Investment Institute's Veronica Willis, an funding method expert, states, "A distinctive portfolio consists of a mixture of belongings that don't continuously pass within the equal direction and the equal significance continually."

8. Up Your Earnings

An vital a part of growing cash is investing in yourself with the aid of increasing your income, even if you can't do it thru an internet brokerage. You have extra money to invest as your profits growth over time. It's the perfect time to start saving for the future if you've been comfortable in your present salary, says Morgan, whether or not or not or now not it is by the use of growing your retirement contributions, paying off debt, or growing an emergency fund. Invest as least half of of of of any pay decorate you get, says monetary manual Michael Kitces, to ensure a cushty retirement. By steadily growing your full-size of dwelling, you make certain that you do no longer fall into the lure of residing at a diploma you can not aid in retirement. If you do no longer agree with you are certified for a merchandising, set up a meeting at the facet of your supervisor to talk about your alternatives for shifting beforehand to your present hobby. In addition, you may need to test out a side industrial company or a passive-profits plan to complement your income.

Ultra-rich making an investment in 2023

Regarding what humans are thinking about now, it is no surprise that inflation has ruled headlines thinking about mid-yr 2021. In the extraordinarily-rich, growing inflation plays a good sized position in their investment picks for the following three hundred and sixty 5 days. There can be processes to look at from the affluent, even if you do not have masses of thousands in the financial group, mainly in mild of the persistent inflationary troubles which have an impact on us all." A take a look at a number of Tiger 21's maximum well-heeled individuals' funding plans for 2023.

1) Building inflation-resistant portfolios

TIGER 21 individuals take into account that inflationary pressures can be in region, and now not quality for a short period as previously notion. About 65% of respondents are expecting inflation will growth next 12 months. To protect towards inflation, they may be making an funding in some of their preferred assets, together with Industrial and industrial institutions, in addition to housing complexes, Platform agencies with price power like Amazon, Apple, and Airbnb, in addition to patron staples and streaming services which might be publicly traded Cryptocurrencies (see No. 2 underneath for extra on this problem depend) It's critical to recall that real assets isn't always absolutely for the wealthy while thinking about inflation-hedging investments. In addition to purchasing for a assets, REITs allow customers to enjoy the actual belongings marketplace (moreover referred to as Real Estate Investment Trusts). We purchase and sell income-producing actual belongings as a REIT employer (shopping for facilities, condominiums, housing developments, hospitals, parking garages, and so forth.)By purchasing REIT stocks, you could get publicity to the REIT's real property belongings at the same time as no longer having to take at the obligation of belongings control yourself. It's feasible to invest in publicly listed REITs like Fidelity through a brokerage account like TD Ameritrade or Robinhood. Still, thru their systems, you can furthermore participate in non-publicly traded REITs like Fundraise, Yieldstreet, or Elevate Money straight away.

2) Doubling their crypto investments

TIGER participants have quadrupled their cryptocurrency investments as an opportunity to buying gold as a hedge in opposition to inflation. In addition to Ethereum (34%), bitcoin (33%), a crypto fund (23%), one-of-a-kind currencies (15%), and dogecoin, TIGER 21 members also are making an investment in the following: (2 percent). These affluent shoppers aren't developing a mistake. Because of its confined amount, Bitcoin is frequently called "digital gold." However, it isn't however easy whether or not or no longer or no longer or no longer Bitcoin can be an powerful inflation hedge in the long run. Investing in cryptocurrency has in no way been much less complicated for the commonplace character manner to the proliferation of monetary programs. The peer-to-peer price app Cash App, owned through Square Inc., most effective lets clients purchase bitcoins. For PayPal customers, there are four varieties of cryptocurrencies to select out from: bitcoin, bitcoin coins (BCH), litecoin, and Ethereum. On the app, clients with cryptocurrency in their PayPal account may additionally moreover use it to pay for goods and services. The well-known dogecoin shaggy dog story cryptocurrency is considered certainly one of seven cryptocurrencies supported by means of the use of using Robinhood, a cellular telephone platform for stock buying and promoting. It's additionally feasible to buy 21 one-of-a-kind crypto tokens and currencies using the SoFi app, a private financial provider. Coinbase allows you to buy, change, alternate, maintain, and transfer over 50 particular sorts of cryptocurrencies proper out of your wallet.

3) Increasing investments in opportunity strength

Tesla, Rivian, and Lucid are though famous investments for the extraordinarily-rich, who are setting extra cash into those groups. You do now not have to buy Tesla stock to obtain publicity to the EV agency through ETFs much like the Global X Autonomous & Electric Vehicles ETF (NASDAQ: DRIV) or the iShares Self-Driving EV and Tech ETF, each of which spend money on a big style of agencies connected to EVs (NYSEMKT: IDRV). It's greater secure to put money into a various portfolio than a single inventory.

Bottom line

Inflation is a tremendous scenario for the rather-rich, so it's fascinating to look how they prepare for the new year. Keeping song of ways extraordinary buyers are guarding towards inflation is a high-quality idea at the same time as you don't forget that it's miles a few component that each investor ought to be considering. The lesson is which you don't want to be a millionaire to stable your coins inside the inventory marketplace. "

The function of technology in powering an Inclusive Future

Additional data belongings are curated for this paper, The Role of Technology in Powering an Inclusive Future, which builds upon the formerly said personal research reports. Its task is to get a global mindset at the have an effect on of era on inclusivity or the diploma to which every body has identical access to the blessings that our societies offer.

1. Create Connection

2. Forge Opportunity

three. Include Everyone

Create Connection

Internet use and reduce tiers of inequality are generally linked, as proven with the resource of a sturdy affiliation among

Internet use and reduced inequality stages. In the last severa a long time, the worldwide availability of era has risen drastically. Moreover, half of the place's populace now has get right of entry to to the Internet as compared with simplest 6.7 percentage in 2000.

Even but, improvement has been erratic. Female Internet clients are, on common, 50% masses much less in all likelihood than male Internet clients to get admission to the Internet, ordinary with the World Economic Forum. Four Similarly, 87.5 percentage of internet data is best available in one of the ten languages spoken in the international. Five This is not their first language, and that's a large a part of the trouble. Only 29 worldwide places provide cheap Internet access. In less-developed nations, ICT use remains largely underneath-consultant of the whole population. In many growing countries, connection infrastructure is still in the early stages of improvement. Modern infrastructure, collectively with roads, trains, energy, and water structures, is becoming more digital. More present day and extra aid-green community manipulate techniques may be used. Many global locations can not use IT because of the fact there is no reliable electric powered grid. Taking care of these foundational worries need to be the number one order of organisation. According to the World Bank, humans residing in rural and underprivileged regions are disproportionately affected by digital divides in greater advanced countries. Examples of countries with broadband utilization just like that of OECD members consist of India, the Kyrgyz Republic, and Moldova's capital. To make topics worse, cell telephone use is shallow in those 3 distant places. These disparities avoid shared prosperity, which prevents people from finding paths out of poverty.

Chapter 11: The price of stepped forward connectivity

To summarize, there may be a high-quality pass lower back on funding in virtual connectivity infrastructure. It is predicted that imparting the Internet to folks who inside the suggest time are disconnected ought to contribute $6.7 trillion to the global economic tool. Eight For example, this may enhance a further 500 million humans out of poverty and display the importance of improving connectedness within the combat in the direction of poverty. This is particularly real even in tons much less advanced global locations, wherein infrastructure is scarce.

2 Forge opportunity

The benefits of connection will most effective be available to those who have obtained the essential training and education; therefore, virtually constructing the important infrastructure will no longer be enough. Because of the facts-primarily based absolutely nature of our contemporary financial tool, that is a especially urgent trouble. People's capability to apply digital generation will more and more decide get admission to to jobs and social services. How properly a country's government can serve its humans is decided with the resource of methods properly it could educate them digitally. To hold the cycle of connectedness, financial opportunity, and inclusion, making an funding in growing human beings's capabilities is crucial. By now not investing in human capital, the World Bank predicts that the productivity of the subsequent generation of employees is probably substantially decreased.

It's critical to discover innovative techniques to invest in personnel. Informal employment employs approximatelybillion people international. Processes inside the production and company industries have become increasingly complicated. However, with the arrival of era, the need for human capabilities is projected to broaden. Producers' information and capabilities may be critical to monetary achievement. Therefore ICT skills are in spite of the fact that inconsistently allotted globally, a exquisite deal as a connection.

Technology for studying

266 million kids worldwide are not capable of flow to school, and 617 million teens are not able to have a study or do primary mathematics. Girls in low-profits international locations are specially uncovered to herbal catastrophes. A actual example of this form of is the Jara Unit, that is designed to deal with this hassle. These solar-powered, wireless portable devices are built to very last. They use games and sports activities culled from instructional databases to teach college students in conventional instructional disciplines. Learning continuity and assistance are supplied at some point of humanitarian

emergencies manner to its advent in some unspecified time in the future of the 2015 earthquake in Nepal. Practical expertise which encompass building a easy plumbing device is also imparted to clients. Local offerings like trauma therapy and microloans also are blanketed.

Technology for talents schooling

Lifelong learning and retraining are already carefully encouraged with the useful resource of technology.

Long-distance reading programs powered by way of way of technology provide personnel a leg up within the undertaking market. Workers may also additionally observe new talents on the same time as keeping their modern-day positions. In the absence of social safety nets, that is critical for displaced workers who have to evolve their capabilities to new employment necessities.

Initiatives like Digital Divide Data assist low-income teenagers in growing global locations. They offer preparation on a manner to acquire success in a digital career. Data enter and record conversion fall beneath this elegance. It is feasible to provide treatments for deprived populations in industrialized economies. Cisco, for example, is a sponsor of Connected North in Canada.

The initiative affords a wide variety of offerings, from far off healthcare advice to on-the-approach training for rural residents.

Addressing international employees gaps

Using era in education and schooling also can furthermore help near the distance among countries concerning ability degrees. For the employee and the close by hard work, this has numerous blessings. A business enterprise's worldwide supply chain can also moreover moreover ultimately be localized through making an funding in training at critical ranges. As a stop end result, worldwide inequality is probably substantially decreased. Eventually, bodily items and assets may be phased out in choice of highbrow property and records. A large effect on inequality in the route of the world could probable stop end end result from this. The employees of current-day rising global places may be included towards the future of their predecessors who labored in superior international places. Manufacturing jobs at the lowest of the rate chain have each been relocated to developing international locations or modified thru technology. Workers may also obtain the blessings of era breakthroughs as their economies and rate chains enhance. It's already possible to make a difference way to modern technologies. Reasonable global solutions are a number of the severa corporations that have partnered with Cisco. Over 750,000 employees in sixteen international locations use Laborlink's platform to post facts on their running situations and education desires. This announcement is a large step in the proper manner for employees to be involved in desire to abused.

three Include all people

It is time to increase the speak on economic inclusion to encompass political and social inclusion.It is feasible to make fitness and social offerings extra extensively to be had through technology. Both countries with horrible healthcare and social-care infrastructure and global locations with mature health and social structures which might be already below pressure are stricken by this.As era advances, healthcare and social services will become extra accessible. Innovations like predictive statistics evaluation and drone era can help increase the blessings of financial boom past the city limits.

Tech-pushed social structures

Extending the obtain of fitness care will need an awareness of close by wishes. This is wherein corporations like OmniVis will make a difference. The biotechnology agency is operating on a transportable tool that would emerge as aware of cholera insects and other ailments in water in as little as half-hour. Cholera is unusual in rich nations, however it impacts an expected 3 million to 5 million people globally who do not have get right of access to to regular ingesting water or sanitary centers. To lessen fatalities and prevent pandemics, early evaluation is essential.

Health structures in industrialized economies are under developing pressure, which serves as a reminder that social structures have to be prolonged-lasting. The development of systems that go through in mind the approaching demographic problems may be made possible through modern, adaptable, technology-based totally, and rate-powerful solutions in growing international locations.

Empowering willing organizations

While a few industrialized international locations conflict to enhance their healthcare systems, new traits that might boom its attraction to Those who're on the outdoor searching in. A few examples: An entrepreneur subsidized through the usage of way of Handisco, Cisco created Herpa. This an clever strolling stick links to a smartphone a metropolis's sensors and statistics prolonged accessibility for oldsters which can be blind or visually impaired cities in France Similar to this is Project It's a awesome price for coins for Vive's Voz Box. A tool that produces speech that allows human beings with speech problems access to schooling is hampered Along with a system. Health care structures are beneath growing pressure. Within the more superior economies, one is reminded social structures need to be Sustainable. The functionality to do multiple matters nicely being reliant on generation, and Affordability is an important interest. The structures that emerge in new economies that preserve in thoughts the demographics worrying situations that lie beforehand The use of generation can empower people. Those who do not in shape the mold Reliant to others' goodwill. They are capable of doing so. Higher than the complicated Historically, huge-scale answers were hired. A time period commonly applied in civil and government circles Society has a obligation to assist parents which can be prone. Communities. Poverty Stoplight, for instance. It is a home development tool. It permits you to accomplish that. Self-assessment for them And rent the belongings available to you nearby. As is everyday, governments hire, issue and teach social employees Workers. They set the bar. Surveying the need for help, observations and specific techniques are hired. Then, they invent and positioned into impact the plan. Solutions. As a end result of the Poverty Stoplight, It is the obligation of a family to examine their situation. Against a 50-object poverty index. Results are depicted in a graph. Dashboard. Then, the family is aided thru a bespoke approach address those issues, as well as Resources are available to residents in the right now vicinity. At the immediately At the equal time, the authorities and the general public useful useful resource companies make the most of their efforts to relieve poverty Insights. They find out if the vicinity is nearby or not. Effectiveness and necessity of property Revision and redoing.

Chapter 12: DOMINATING THE GAME OF WEALTH

It is a activity to Earn coins. Mainly, fine human beings hold the strings at the same time as others are the manikins. The tomfoolery component is that you can conclude which aspect of the sport you need to be on - the puppeteer or the manikin.

Nobody inside the international come to be conceived fortunate. Everybody 'lucky' that you may accept as true with - the maximum extravagant people on earth possibly - weren't conceived fortunate. Concurred that a element of these people were brought into the area to rich households and in wealthy homes, but we as a whole realise that that is not sufficient to get topics going.

The truth of the trouble is that those humans have dominated the spherical of abundance in a while in their lives. They may want to conceivably have been brought into the arena with the cash, however they have got discovered a manner to play the coins undertaking.

Individuals talk a ton approximately the round of abundance without sincerely information what it implies. Throughout everyday lifestyles, we want to place in some thing to get some factor. Indeed, no matter cash it's miles that manner. If you have any desire to herald cash, you want to location in something. This is probably a financial hypothesis or it thoroughly may be some one-of-a-kind shape of challenge like a hypothesis of time or exertion or a particular ability or notion, and so on. However, the reality of the problem is that some thing want to be contributed.

Be that as it is able to, there can be a amazing deal of assessment in what people make a contribution. Certain individuals may need to make contributions a wonderful deal however get very little, whilst there are likewise folks that make a contribution barely some factor however get a ton. These people apprehend the manner to take advantage of what they have got. They understand a way to region in barely some detail and get what the superb majority on the planet can be in wonderment of. These are humans who've ruled the round of riches.

The first-rate aspect is that the round of abundance isn't out of benefit and neither is it unreachable. Anybody can modify oneself to turn into an professional at this game. Anything their ongoing situation is, they may go their lives toward large cash. You can do it as properly. What you actually need is the proper mentality, the right approach and a pair of diverse topics. This is in that you start.

NOBODY IS BROUGHT INTO THE WORLD WITH THE KNOWLEDGE OF BECOMING RICH

The facts on becoming rich comes on in the future down the road. This is the way you may acquire your education spherical proper right here.

We have proactively expressed how people are in no way delivered into the arena with their lavishness. They may be really introduced to lavishness, but this extravagance isn't theirs. Assuming they need to make it their very very very own, they want to paintings for it.

It's glaringly real that a wealthy man may be in addition as involved approximately his little one as an unlucky man could be. The of them might determine how their youngsters may oversee subjects once they became older. The most important problem right proper here is - Every man desires to pursue wealth. They aren't added into the arena with the statistics.

Ponder one of the maximum extravagant men of our instances - Bill Gates. The toddler of a modest lawyer and a trainer nowadays has a whole asset of forty billion bucks, making him the maximum extravagant coins manager within the international. All his abundance has come from a solitary deliver - Microsoft - which in itself is one of the maximum powerful businesses of the area in any age and period.

Do you expect Bill Gates become counseled uniquely in evaluation to maximum of us? Is it actual that he turned into a greater tremendous youngster than the the rest? No, as a depend of fact. Indeed, he have become an understudy at Harvard, however he left his schooling halfway to searching out after his commercial enterprise (which have become Microsoft). In reality, he modified into as quickly as tested via his educator for his lazy nature, while he replied that he might accumulate his initial million previous he hit a long term vintage. Indeed, Bill Gates acquired his preliminary billion preceding he arrived at 21 years antique.

So, what placed him aside? Something that made him particular round then grow to be that he understood what he had to do. He didn't permit the razzle-stun of his massive call college fluster him. He maintained his interest on what drove him. He liaised with the correct people; those who he knew have to take him earlier and who he have to take beforehand within the device as properly. He stayed sincere to himself about his economic position and he vowed to himself to enhance.

Yet, in particular, Bill Gates did not successfully ponder cash!

He rather pondered the individual of his object. He requested himself again and again, "Is the difficulty I am giving going to do anything to the arena?" That placed him aside. We generally assume, "Will this create a advantage for me?", at the same time as folks who accomplish lavishness suppose, "Will this gain the region?"

What's extra, this statistics does not come upon moving into the area. You recognize this as you increase, further as you take a look at different things. You find out that extravagance does now not drop by using deliberating coins; as a depend of reality, that makes the contrary distinction.

What to keep in mind right right right here is that no individual is delivered into the arena with the statistics on turning into rich. You discover that as you boom, in a similar way as you decorate such countless numerous topics. However, what really makes you rich is wearing out this records on the proper second for your existence.

Chapter 13: THE MINDSET OF THE RICH

The rich psyche should suppose uniquely in evaluation to the middleclass care. Indeed, the statistics confirm that extravagance stays inside the psyche and no longer inside the monetary organization stability.

It can be very a good buy a reality that the wealthy brain thinks in an unexpected manner. They have a vastly amazing perspective from the meant middleclass and the destitute person's thoughts. We have formerly introduced a brief test out that. The rich person's brain ponders giving brilliant than approximately acquiring their private benefit. They ponder how their gadgets advantage society. This is the very issue that motives people to location inventory in what they supply and purchase the ones topics. Making people purchase their object is probably of the maximum un-hassle in the wealthy man or woman's psyche.

There are one in every of a kind features that exemplify the wealthy character's mind. One of those is the management characteristics that they've. Glance round - each unmarried rich guy and women of this present reality are pioneers right here and there or the other. The majority of them are heads of state or stand corporation on every other such footing of pressure. A ton of them are cash managers and financial professionals who order round a hundred people each day. A few of them are VIPs inside the realm of films and game; even the ones people are pioneers thru their very very own doing because of the reality they rule the sector to which they have got a place.

The other first rate is charm. Without that, wealth does not befit an person. The individual should have the choice to hold their wealth. They should have the selection to radiate the expertise from being rich. They need to have an inspirational attitude.

In any case, what is the motivation at the back of being rich assuming that you are forced over your price range?

Rich humans likewise ponder generosity and noble reason. Each man or woman this is rich is engaged with many reasons; the more a part of them have installation NGOs and exceptional such establishments to assist the bulk. This indicates their social streak. All matters taken into consideration, each single wealthy man and girls emerge from a herbal longing to perform some thing useful for the general public, whether or not or no longer that is thru their organisation gadgets or via their magnanimous deeds.

To be a wealthy person, you want to begin questioning like one. This is wherein you want to start changing your person. Peruse histories of the pinnacle rich

Chapter 14: RICH PEOPLE GENERALLY THINK NORTHWARD

Individuals who have arrived at their zeniths of final outcomes in our contemporary global share one detail almost speaking - they've got in no way pondered a few component quick of the excellent.

One ordinary extraordinary that you may music down about the rich human beings in this gift fact or on every occasion is they in no way count on little. Rich people will generally ponder the most important, the greatest, the maximum amazing, the maximum extravagant, and plenty of others. In addition to that, they devise in them a preeminent reality that they will accomplish their idea method. This separates them. Rich people commonly take a gander on the north, the real top of success.

If you've got got any desire to gain wealth, you want to copy this perspective simply. You need to regulate your brain's compass in the path of the north as nicely. You need to count on beyond practical barriers; you want to assume that you can accomplish what you are that specialize in. Assume that your existence's desire is to claim a chain of 5-superstar lodges, however you do not for even a 2d have valid cash in your room lease at the existing time. Would or no longer it's a extremely good idea a excellent manner to virtually brush this choice to the most profound openings of your thoughts, letting your self recognize that you could never accomplish it?

Not the slightest bit! All subjects taken into consideration; you want to paintings in your self the know-how that you may accomplish. You want to expect that this will rise up. At the problem even as you hold that attitude - while your work in your self the outright self belief that this will arise - it's going to certainly exercising consultation.

Believe there can be no truth on this? Indeed, hold in mind it yet again! How about we take the hotels preference model. Regardless of whether or not or not or no longer you're dwelling in a leased room at the prevailing time, in the occasion that you truly need mission your accommodations ultimately, and assuming that you spend constantly mulling over the entirety and every drowsing second dreaming about it, then you definately actually truely are glaringly heading to study steps in the course of fun your choice. Each step which you steer may be a stage that manner, whether or not or now not it's far saving a $one hundred in line with week or whether or not or not or now not it is looking for economic help from banks some years down the line. Assuming that your aspiration is overpowering, you can in all truth do stuff to get it going.

It works. Rich people have set up that this type of aggressive reasoning works. How approximately Donald Trump have been the aggregate he is these days assuming he had been contenting along alongside together with his most memorable singular business enterprise? Do you suppose Bill Gates might have been the maximum extravagant character on this present truth at the off chance that he had waited with the fruitful BASIC programming he deliberate with Paul Allen? Not in any respect. It is at the same time as you recall that the ones humans concept inside the direction of the north and persevered to expect that way that they had been given the success they generally longed for.

UNSHACKLE YOUR THOUGHTS FROM YOUR CIRCUMSTANCES

Most instances, you're your very own adversary. You restrict making yourself wealthy. You want to conquer yourself to a degree to get that wealth.

Perhaps you have got a really powerful urge of turning into pretty possibly of the most extravagant man or woman the area has seen but probable you're hindering yourself. Have you at any element belief along the accompanying traces: -

•"How would in all likelihood I at any thing arrive at the fulfillment the ones Forbes human beings have reached?"

•"How should I, a person with a $500 salary, grow to be a rich character?"

•"I could not myth approximately becoming wealthy in slight of the reality that no person in my own family has at any issue been rich."

•"I'm not equipped to pay even my rent. How should probable I buy an extravagance yacht?"

See what you're doing? You are allowing your self to restrict you. You are not liberating your most capability due to the fact you determine you can't make it take location. You have some situations at some stage in regular lifestyles - everyone has -

which you think will keep you from getting at that multitude of wealth we're speakme approximately. Yet, on the off risk that you have a have a look at life testimonies of the most extravagant humans in this present truth, you may locate that a very critical degree of them have ascended from ghettos, trash dumps, ghettos, once more rear entryways, and masses of others. A superb deal of them have now not had cash to eat as soon as. A ton of their families haven't seen a $a hundred together besides at Christmas.

Do you honestly determine you can not make it appear? Recall that no person is truly delivered to wealth - now not even the children of the maximum extravagant people in recent times. Everybody wishes to make the maximum of in all likelihood difficult conditions a manner to guide their abundance or to a manner to accumulate it. That is the motive you want to free up yourself from yourself.

Quit imagining that you cannot accomplish at the grounds which you are of an change religion, an exchange tone, an change social basis, one-of-a-kind instructive functionality, a bodily or highbrow take a look at or no distinction both manner. History has examined again and again that suffering breeds achievement. You will be the following poverty to newfound wealth story at the Forbes.

Do you have your psyche set on becoming wealthy? Do you have got that one capacity you consider you studied the world surely care approximately? Is it genuine that you are as of now a chunk call to your little market? Is it regular to mention which you are tremendous of becoming rich? In the occasion that genuinely, you need to put forth the attempt surely. Recollect that lavishness can emerge out of everywhere.

Chapter 15: BEFRIEND MONEY

Cash might be the maximum specifically awful rumored element in our reality. In any case, the fact of the problem is, coins makes lifestyles as we're aware of it feasible.

How often have you ever ever heard terrible dating with coins in our everyday day language? Consider the ones...

•On the off hazard which you have cash, you emerge as covetous.

•Needs are not often satisfied.

•Cash does now not fall from the sky.

•No will increase without torments.

•Cash makes misleading companions.

This is our ordinary language. However, taking a gander at those articulations, it sincerely does appear to be that cash is a totally horrible element, proper? Nobody ought to have a pleasing impression of cash at the off hazard that they may be recommended with these proclamations.

Truth be knowledgeable, this is the justification for why the greater element humans of the arena are stalled with the useful resource of troubles regarding coins. Why, we ought to say the share of humans with economic issues want to be appreciably larger than that! We study such pessimistic courting about cash that we start feeling that cash is a in truth terrible trouble.

Our parents, instructors, strict evangelists, otherworldly masters, everyone allow us to recognize that money is extraordinarily awful. However, at that point even the ones human beings are in the sport for the coins, accurate? We foster one of these terrible factor of view approximately cash from our youngsters from those humans that over the direction of lifestyles we do not recollect it well. What's greater, while we develop up, we skip in this mantle of contempt in the direction of coins to our kids and that they develop up detesting it as nicely.

The outcome - one monetarily limited age brings forth each other.

We really need to save you this cycle at the prevailing time. We actually need to remove this quite misguided view approximately coins that we're benefited from. We need to warmth up to coins.

Cash in fact allows financial life on earth. Without it, now not a solitary button must alternate palms. We have fabricated the world on the inspiration of coins and presently it's miles in fact no longer viable that we are able to take off from it.

Try not to look coins as your adversary. This is pessimists' forte. These are those who have not introduced in coins in their lives or probably have acquired such pretty some that it does no longer depend in any respect to them irrespective of whether or not or now not others do.

You want to reinforce your very own condition. It is time you befriended coins.

GOD MAINTAINS THAT US SHOULD BE RICH

Assuming that money have been underhanded, for what reason will we examine God with overflow?

All thru the Book of Genesis, we have some fashions that God loves overflow. The actual Garden of Eden that God assembled emerge as the embodiment of greater. Everything become sufficient for Man in that nursery and God asked us to scrutinize it brazenly.

Our depraved deeds were given us expelled from the Garden of Eden, but that did now not prevent God from following us to the way of lavishness. On the off danger that you take a look at through the stories of Abraham, Noah, Moses and David; you recognize how God believed people have to be wealthy. He even gifted them with topics therefore of their remarkable deeds. God compensated Man with wealth. Then, might likely our God at any factor be toward us turning into rich?

Certain people with personal stake curve religion. They speak approximately God being toward wealth. They even project to such an excessive as to mention that accumulating cash is conflicting with the Word of God. All matters considered, assuming that had been the scenario, for what reason will we generally guarantee that God is the maximum extravagant and maximum massive detail in the Universe?

The truth of the hassle is that God loves human beings being altruistic. Furthermore, noble purpose comes evidently at the off threat that you are rich. God comprehends that Man want to be happy to be huge-hearted. Just even as Man can fill his very very own cup would likely he at any difficulty allow it to spill over to specific humans. In the occasion that God has made Man sincerely in His picture, and assuming God is relatively rich, could not He preserve that Man need to be in addition as well?

We were given over a completely twisted view about faith as respects cash. As an extended way as we is probably concerned, it's miles critical to dispose of this bogus shroud we had been approached to wear and be aware matters as they'll be. Maybe, the Reformation development have turn out to be unfinished. They have to have added on individuals to recognize that God is not inside the course of bringing in cash, however that He is in the direction of concerning coins inside the incorrect manner.

Assuming you begin imagining that our God believes us should emerge as wealthy, you can see that you therefore begin moving inside the route of becoming wealthy.

Chapter 16: THE RICH CREATE OPEN DOORS THUMP AT THEIR DOOR

Potential open doorways do not come your course constantly. That's what you apprehend. However, with the rich, this proverb could now not paintings. A truly fruitful guy is an individual who can track down an open door and apprehend its proper potential. Indeed, open doors in fact do thump past times at an effective person's entryway.

Valuable open doors don't thump instances. How often have you heard it stated? Be that as it can, do you truely anticipate this saying is legitimate?

The reality is that you could create open doorways thump at your entryway however generally as you want. Haven't you mentioned about humans who have turn out to be fruitful, then, at that aspect, burnt out, and in a while resurged to grow to be higher than all people may moreover have expected? It takes area continuously round us. Open doorways don't drop thru best a single time. Be that as it may, to make them come to you time and again, you want a few competencies.

Figuring out Opportunities

First and principal, you need to understand what an 'possibility' signifies. Very similar to God, wonderful open doorways are available one-of-a-kind sizes and patterns as properly. A fundamental email address may be your chance. A assembly card mendacity right inside the the front of you unclaimed is probably your chance. A night time at the shopping for middle will be your danger since you can meet anybody precise. Truly, you need to not make moderate of some thing. Anything can turn your lifestyles to enhance topics.

Review Value

Now and once more, you really need to head back and count on. You need to don't forget subjects. At the factor whilst you meet a herbal face out of nowhere out and approximately, inside the event that you could right away positioned them, they'll be so dazzled with you that they welcome you for an agreement. A first rate memory generally makes a difference. You will see that everybody in fee have splendid memories. Get into some reminiscence constructing practices on the off threat that you're not gifted with a characteristic splendid memory.

Never Saying "Bite the dust"

The big majority who meet with disappointment as quickly as are obligated to enjoy that they will no longer ever succeed any greater. To add to that, there are a few doubters surrounding them who usually inform they will not have the choice to upward push inside the future. In any case, you clearly want to do not show homage others' belief method. You want to make sure that each other open door is probably discovered and you can end up higher.

Look constantly for Opportunities

Typically, at the equal time as a person exhibits that they have got determined a few detail superb, they give up searching for whatever extra. Most in all likelihood, you are now into an powerful venture. At the factor at the same time as the sort of situation is available, you're very great to take a gander at something else cautiously. Notwithstanding, you need to make certain that you do not give up looking. Perhaps, every other open door will come your path and taking it up can make you extra extravagant than you have been previously. Investigate Donald Trump, or any fruitful financial professional so far as that is worried. They as of now have their very personal profoundly robust agencies. However, does that prevent them from checking outstanding roads out? They are constantly enhancing, and giving their new open doors the very power that they gave their initial one.

These four trends assure that the open doors come continuously to you. You benefit from one cohesion to some other. This pushes you on.

OFFERING IN RETURN

You really want to provide in move back assuming you actually need to get extra. This is the crucial problem regulation of nature. It works no change way.

We see this anywhere spherical us. On the ranch, for instance. At the detail even as the rancher reaps his yield, he flora returned a portion of the seeds into the residence. These seeds will assist him with getting more harvest. You see what is going on - The rancher is presenting returned a few component of what he receives. This guarantees that he receives greater.

See Bill Gates himself. He is the organizer behind quite probably of the maximum crucial magnanimous affiliation in the world, the Bill and Melinda Gates Foundation. This enterprise works in a few global places, each one of the nations that he has made his wealth from. He is providing in pass returned. At the thing whilst that is what he does, human beings experience far higher approximately him. This assists him with uniting his state of affairs. Obviously, that isn't always his notion at the same time as he's sporting out some thing useful for great human beings, but that is the way in which it clearly works, right?

Investigate any superstar, any industrialist, everyone who is getting alongside well. In their personal unique way, everybody is along with to a purpose or the alternative.

For what cause could they may be pronouncing they are doing that? For what purpose do not they honestly swarm all the abundance that they have and dismiss the arena? That is for the reason that at the identical time as you grow to be wealthy, you pay attention that profound inward voice advising you to offer in go back. At the difficulty at the same time as you do, you enjoy far higher approximately it. You see the overflow streaming. You gain strength from the inclination which you have given a few element decrease lower back to humans who have helped make you wealthy.

Storing is the thoughts-set of horrific humans. Offering again is the mind-set of the rich.

At the point at the same time as you provide in cross returned, you could connect with the ones who have to help you with turning into greater grounded. This commonly works. In this global, charitableness is the route to progress.

DOING YOUR ABSOLUTE BEST

A mentality of being wealthy has been depicted with the useful resource of the media as a contemptible outlook. Why would likely that be? Does the perpetual longing to grow to be rich mean which you are realistic?

Frequently, we've got visible people being spoken unwell about because of the fact that they want to emerge as wealthy. "Cash is all that is at the forefront of his mind," "He will do something for cash,"... such are the discussions we find out approximately them. That can also additionally need to prevent some oldsters from going into useful endeavors. A few of us get the feeling that it is some detail horrendous to ponder cash.

In any case, there's some factor you have to be aware - It is not bringing in coins this is terrible. It is the way in which certain people do it this is terrible.

You need to grow to be wealthy. And yet you want to look what charges you need to pay for it. Is it real or now not that you have become wealthy to the detriment of creating an funding energy at the side of your circle of relatives? Might or not it's stated which you have end up wealthy putting a few harmless humans in question? Assuming you are doing that, you're malicious. However, at the off risk that you are bringing in cash thru honorable strategies and, helping others with doing that as well, then you definitely definitely are doing it the right way. This is the way in that you deliver in coins and ensure you manual it as properly.

Chapter 17: Get Rich: Yes YOU Can

There are only some people on this international who wouldn't want to be rich. Having the coins to stay lifestyles to the fullest, content material fabric with all your coronary coronary coronary heart's goals, is sort of a dream. But, for a select few, that dream can emerge as a truth. Not, it is not the success of the draw that determines who will make it to the fame of millionaire or wealthy. It is reserved for folks who understand what it takes to end up wealthy, people who have the choice to get to be had and get it. Sitting round looking, hoping or being afraid isn't going to accumulate outcomes.

You are liable for your personal existence. Perhaps a bit cliché and some difficulty which you have heard 1,000,000 times over, but clearly some factor that jewelry with every little little bit of truth inside the again of it. Sitting around questioning that it is not the time to take action, that you do not have what it takes or hoping that a few element is going to trade is doing not some thing extra than losing precious time. If you need a few factor in life then it's far as a whole lot as you to exit there and get it. Yes, it genuinely is that smooth. If you are not willing to make the number one steps then there can be now not some thing else that would show up. It is vital that you assume topics through and determine what lifestyles you want to live. If it is nicely well worth making adjustments and getting to the to you'll be capable of locate all that you need to get there.

The cause that so many human beings are stuck struggling and of their present day manner of existence and scenario is due to the reality they aren't doing what they need to do to get to the top. They wish and dream massive, and that is all first rate and dandy. But it takes motion to get consequences. It takes desire and pressure, and compassion and willingness. And once more, it is an extended way greater of a complicated scenario than virtually doing a pair of factors to make a bit little little bit of cash. In order to get rich it takes unique making plans, hobby to detail, and sure, so frequently it takes sacrifice, too.

Steps To Make Yourself Rich

SO, what do you want to do to accomplish that and begin taking walks your manner to the top of the economic ladder?

If feasible, discover a mentor, or on the minimum take a look at what successful human beings have finished to get to the pinnacle. Whether it's far Jimmy Buffet, Steve Jobs or maybe the Trump that you idolize in approach of financial repute, you can research masses from those human beings (and others) through studying their tale. And, a mentor offers even more arms-on leisure. Although you can't be running with a call just like the Donald, the ones who've attained millionaire recognition are powerful to offer you with all that you want for achievement.

Decide what you will do to come to be wealthy, and description the quantity of cash which you need. Simply bringing up that you want to grow to be rich isn't a clean enough purpose, as you could spend the the relaxation of your life seeking to 'get wealthy 'with out a clean definition of what which means to you. Know how a bargain cash you need to earn, the way you recommend to get the cash, and the date in that you need to have it pay. Along with imparting motivation, having definitive dollar amounts and dates can provide encouragement and steering to help you attain the location that you want to be in lifestyles.

Stop procrastinating and looking ahead to the great timing. There is in no way going to be an extremely good time to jump on the bandwagon, and if you in no manner get began out you'll by no means have a shot at making it wealthy. If you have have been given clean mind of what you need, a manner to get it and are unafraid of any disturbing situations that could stand to your way, it is honestly the right time so you can begin.

Is it the worry of failure that has stopped you from taking the subsequent steps? If so, you aren't on my own. Many human beings locate this to be a barrier once they want to emerge as rich. What occurs if I fail? Will human beings look down upon me? How can I ever try once more after a failure? Another key to becoming wealthy and a success is to recognize that failure is part of existence. We make mistakes. But, with each mistake that is made we've a observe from it. And, even as we analyze we're able to develop and drift at once to larger and higher subjects. You mustn't allow the concern of not being a fulfillment, or of making mistakes along the way, prevent you from greatness. If you're making a mistake, it takes location. No one is pleasant, or perhaps the crème of the croup names have made errors alongside the direction to their fortune. They have placed and moved past them, and remembering this is important in your fulfillment.

If you need to end up rich, that is a ball that is on your court docket. Which way will you dribble the ball? If you're willing to plan, alternate the manner which you anticipate and make investments a while and energy, that ball can be in the proper court docket and achievement may be for your destiny. It is as much as you and what you are inclined to do. Does turning into wealthy endorse that a good deal to you? If it does, getting at the ball and getting with this gadget is your subsequent step. You have the strength to turn out to be wealthy. Anyone does. Anyone.

Chapter 18: The Road To Riches

Now that you apprehend what it takes to stroll the street to economic fulfillment, it's time to discover how you may walk on that road. Or, you need to determine what you may do to get rich and begin making smart moves financially and otherwise. There are many methods that you can select to make investments your cash. It isn't without a tremendous deal of time and brainstorming that you ought to pick your technique. Do research on the thoughts that come into your mind, mastering what's worthwhile and what is not. Ensure which you are searching at things which can be thrilling to you as properly. Although making an investment or getting wealthy isn't normally fun, it's miles feasible to find out some aspect this is at least relatively interesting to you. It is a ways a great deal much less complex to preserve to your efforts of having rich when you are playing what you're doing.

You can locate many techniques to investigate and analyze what is and what isn't always going to be genuinely virtually really worth your at the same time as. Keep in mind the amount of time that you need to invest in becoming rich and your real hopes for purchasing there. Will you open a commercial company? Are you someone inquisitive about buying and selling stocks? These are really a number of the techniques that you could make your self rich.

It is essential that you additionally alternate your mindset. If you need to get wealthy you need to think like a wealthy man or woman. It doesn't take exquisite amounts of cash to attain this fame in life, and every single penny counts. Learn the manner to expect correctly approximately cash. It will alternate your complete attitude approximately spending, help you emerge as greater aware about wherein your coins is going and assist you're making greater sound alternatives even as it's time to make investments your coins the right way.

As noted inside the ultimate financial ruin it's also crucial that you save you looking ahead to the right time to do subjects due to the reality that point is in no manner going to go back. There will usually be challenges which is probably status in the manner, topics that surely do no longer seem proper. However, those aren't some thing extra than excuses, and people who're a hit are in fact now not people which is probably making excuses. Get it all together, and even as you revel in that your mind is inside the proper vicinity and that you have the choice to get to be had and get it, you have got observed the proper time to begin.

Write out your plans. No, thinking it isn't sufficient. By developing a marketing approach you are assisting your self in a number of strategies. First, you gained't forget something, or any of the stairs that have to be taken to get there. Second, have to you be making plans to open a industrial enterprise or want top notch varieties of monetary assist, having the advertising and marketing approach in vicinity will assist you get the coins this is needed. Another gain of writing thins out is that it is able to provide you with steering and motivation every day of the week. You will by no means overlook about really what it is which you are striving for whilst it is there in simple sight if you need to appearance.

At the pinnacle of this paper, create a completely unique assertion, a phrase of motivation or encouragement that you can have a look at aloud each day to offer motivation your manner. Our brains are very special, and on the same time as you inform yourself a few detail enough instances in the end you can recollect it to be real. It is with that thoughts-set that you are virtually capable of wearing out outstanding matters on this existence, on the aspect of the financial reputation you are after.

Get obtainable and meet others who proportion inside the identical dreams as you. There are lots of groups available in lots of big towns, however in case you aren't any close, don't worry, as there may be moreover masses of first-rate help which may be attained online. Having help and being round nicely appropriate individuals can assist for your success at the identical time as moreover supplying you an abundance of information, recommendations and plenty greater.

Saving coins as fast as possible is likewise a step that would assist fill the bank account. Always assume two instances before developing a buy, although it is a small object that costs only a few bucks. Those bucks can speedy add up and earlier than you recognise it you have got spent more than what became intended. Besides, getting wealthy will by no means display up in case you are a large spender. Until you obtain the fortune that you want in existence it's miles crucial to recall which you need to live your manner of lifestyles, not the only of what you open for in the future. Save every penny that you may, and in no way hesitate to look for strategies to make extra money on what you have got already got.

Resisting temptation is difficult, so be organized for it to be difficult occasionally. That dress which you have constantly favored at 80% off is an splendid deal, absolutely because the airline tickets for a extraordinary cheap charge. But, is it sincerely without a doubt well worth it? What will you need with the dress? What brilliant charges come even as you board the airline? There isn't always any stone left exposed while you're on the road to riches, so make certain which you recognize in which each unmarried penny which you have is going.

Chapter 19: Get Rich: Tips For Success

Now that you apprehend what it takes to acquire the fortune that you choice, check the ones recommendations that will help you get to the top and locate the adamant amount of fulfillment which you are searching out.

1.Don't be Afraid to be Different: If you go along with what all and sundry else is doing, how will you anticipate to get results any character-of-a-type than what they may be? In order to get to the top, to get wealthy and be the wonderful that you may be it takes being special, doing subjects simply a chunk in a considered one of a kind manner than what really anyone else is doing. The essential thing to don't forget right right here is which you shouldn't be afraid to be specific and to do matters which you are confident gets you in advance.

2.Stop Listening to Naysayers: There will constantly be folks that doubt you, folks who want to look you fail, and in all likelihood even those who do their damndest to see you fail. You can not be aware of those those who let you know which you are making the incorrect alternatives, that you could in no way make it, and so forth. Some humans are jealous to appearance what special humans can do due to the fact they need this for themselves. But, in place of amidst this they pick out to rain on precise people's parades. You can not stop their actions or their phrases, however you can choose not to pay attention to them. If you have the selection in your coronary coronary heart to make it to the top, and positioned your terms into moves you can get in that you need to be!

3.Depending on Loans is a No No: It is good enough to help your self with minimal amounts of loans that may be repaid if it's miles clearly essential. Otherwise keep away from them. This is particularly actual for large portions of coins. Once you come to be snug getting loans you're apt to do it over and over. Sometimes sufficient is virtually in no manner enough. But, the skinny about loams, is that they ought to be repaid, and usually the interest expenses on the loans is excessive so that you are paying lower lower returned an extended manner extra than you surely borrowed.

4.Learn to Barter: When you're making an investment in real possession, be it a present day day apparel line or a few difficulty else, discover ways to barter, and apprehend which you have the pinnacle hand inside the deal. You have what they need. The ball is for your court docket docket docket, and also you need to constantly step as tons as any address the attitude of knowledge you are honestly in charge. Now, this isn't to mention you need to end up an evil and no longer feasible man or woman shouting out call for after call for. But, you want to not continuously accept the primary offer that comes along, nor ought to you be afraid to talk your mind and what you want out of the deal. The most a success human beings in this international are those who realise their price and significance and aren't afraid to move after that.

5.Put Away the Cards: Just as you do now not want to come to be based totally upon loans to help you in the road to achievement, you furthermore mght want to pull away from credit rating gambling playing cards as thousands as feasible. While they are not loans, they are capable of reason actually as plenty hassle and make it harder to ever accumulate the rich popularity in existence that you are hoping for. Credit playing cards supply with them big interest charges and people upload up. Unless an emergency, live away from the use of the plastic as frequently as you possibly can do.

6.It is Okay to Quit: Depending at the form of investments which you are making, there can be risks worried. And, in a few conditions you may decrease returned out at the equal time as you do no longer see that topics are moving into your pick out. It is much like the on-line on line casino. When you're on a winning streak you hold going. But, as soon as the odds start to roll from your preference, you stroll away, as a minimum in case you need to maintain your coins. This identical rule of thumb applies whilst making investments and in search of to get wealthy. When it doesn't appear proper, whilst you are losing greater than what you're prevailing, even as you don't revel in right approximately the situation to any quantity in addition, back out. It is ok. It does now not endorse that you are a failure or that some thing is incorrect with you, nor does it advise that your chance of riches is long long gone all the time. This is truly a way of clever inventory and a method that works!

7.Understand the Risks: Do no longer count on that you could discover a risk-free manner of turning into rich. I do not accept as proper with that this form of thing exists. But, what does exist is the potential to assess all the conditions and the dangers which might be involved with the scenario. When you are aware of the functionality dangers you could do everything in your energy to relieve issues and ensure that you are making all the clever selections with the least amount of risks.

eight.The Little stuff topics: Every unmarried penny that you spend topics. Every choice that you make subjects. Do not ever expect that it's miles too small of a desire to count number. When you have got goals in location and want to trade life as you apprehend it, the small things clearly do rely. Whether cash or some factor else, the selections which you make could have an effect on you significantly, so continually located the equal quantity of idea and attention into the small selections as what you do the large ones.

9.Respect your Money: Respecting your coins also can seem like an exceptional trouble to mention however it is one this is proper. You need to recognize your cash. What you have got in addition to what you'll make, too. If you understand your coins it'll be spent, invested and handled well.

10. Do not give up: Giving up may seem like the issue to do while subjects aren't going wrong, even as excellent human beings round you're pronouncing that you'll by no means make it and on the equal time as exclusive mishaps get up. But, this isn't the issue to do, and giving up need to no longer be a preference for your existence. It takes time, it takes persistence and persistence, and sometimes there can be topics that take vicinity alongside the manner. You want to in reality recoup at the same time as awful subjects take area, test and grow and circulate ahead. You are regarded aware about what you shouldn't do and may try to do better within the destiny. But, regardless

of what you do, by no means surrender for your desires.

These are just a number of the recommendations that may be used to help you get wealthy and stay that way. If you're someone this is critical about making extra cash than a hint bit, the use of those hints is some detail that you in fact ought to do.

Chapter 20: Staying Rich: What It Takes To Maintain Your Wealth

You made it. You're a success and function a ton of cash stashed within the financial institution account. But, it can all be long long past within the blink of a watch constant in case you are not careful. So many people make it to the extent of achievement they've got dreamed of, simplest to be blind to the way to preserve that degree of achievement. It is genuinely tough to get a taste then need to allow it skip. Instead, take a look at those hints that will help you discover ways to hold directly to the coins which you have positioned as opposed to be once more inside the identical catch 22 situation in a few short years. Use all of these recommendations to your benefit and you won't be missing out on any of the coins and the rewards.

First and critical, don't begin spending your cash like loopy. Just as you controlled it nicely earlier than fulfillment, now which you have located it, taking the identical care is a need to. This is a few different place in which such a lot of human beings fail. They experience the enjoy of empowerment and pleasure whilst there's now extra cash around. But, just as rapid as that money got here it can be taken away, too. Rather than take the cash that you have made and exit on a buying spree, look for strategies that you can make extra money and keep earning off of your investments.

Continue making investments and seeking out greater techniques to characteristic to the cash which you have. It isn't enough to grow to be rich and prevent in all of your efforts. Money will now not final all the time, regardless of how careful you are. As lengthy as you preserve for your endeavors to make cash, to turn out to be wealthy, the coins will maintain to go along with the glide in. You aren't caught with truely one opportunity, both, so do now not count on that your alternatives are restricted. Most of the maximum a success people on this world have now not stuck with sincerely one manner of having coins. Take a search for your self. Many singers flip to acting, they carry about out new traces of perfume and cologne and of path garb. Some invest, others do industrial spots. There are such a variety of methods to make cash and to hold which includes to the quantity which you have. When you are flexible and open to all of those alternatives you could honestly make extra cash than what you ever expected in advance than. Do no longer experience which you are stuck with in reality one possibility or that you cannot mission out. Although it's far a chance, if you are preserving the method that helped you to get wealthy within the first place then you definately definately are aware about what you ought to and need to now not be doing.

Once you're technically rich make sure that you have a financial adviser working for you if you have not already went this course and decided a person that will help you on this department. A economic adviser is an person who's expert and quite professional at coping with a massive form of economic dreams. They can make sure that you are making the proper economic choices and help you preserve higher tune of each penny which you spend. As we have already mentioned, it is not clearly the big subjects that remember. Every penny you spend, and ultimately every choice which you make has an effect to your lifestyles and what the final consequences of things may be. The rate of hiring a monetary adviser will variety, but you can assume for it to be an investment well sincerely worth the coins. The extra cash that you need to govern the more difficult that it turns into, and for optimum human beings dealing with this on my own is the final issue they want to do. Thanks to the first rate assist provided via a monetary adviser this is no longer a call for.

Chapter 21: Richest People In The World

Warren Buffet is one of the richest men inside the worldwide. Currently Mr. Buffet has a fortune actually well worth $sixty two billion. The 80 three-3 hundred and sixty five days-antique inventory man started out out making investments again in 1962. He did matters proper, this is for sure, and now he has masses of bragging rights. Buffet says that his fulfillment came from the usage of numerous special strategies, which we've got stated on this manual.

Bill Gates, a name that everyone recognize, helped flip era round and into what we recognize it to be nowadays. Gates is the founder of Microsoft, if you were locked in a cave somewhere and did no longer already understand that. Gates presently has a net well well worth of $77 billion bucks, and that amount keeps to rise.

Larry Ellision is every different one of the worldwide's richest men. Ellision is the founding father of the Oracle vacuum cleanser, and a clever man he's. Currently simply well worth truly over $50 billion, Ellision is a race automobile cause stress who has took his cash and made many smart investments through the years.

Kirk Kerkorian is genuinely certainly worth round $750 million. His cash and claim to popularity came through the hole of his many casinos and clever investment options being made at some point of the development of those casinos. The 96 12 months vintage MGM Grand founder, no matter his age, remains available seeking out techniques to make money, and he appears to though have it, continuing to growth his profits and internet well well worth on a every day basis.

We all recognize how masses cash other famous names have —like Oprah Winfrey and the sports activities massive name and buyers. It is really not the nice fortune of the draw and people human beings did no longer without a doubt get fortunate. They worked tough and once they positioned their opportunity they pounced in to tough and fast. You should be prepared to pounce, too.

What do all of these men, and the numerous other billionaires and millionaires in the worldwide have in common? They have been all adamant approximately what they desired in existence and have been not afraid to move after it. Each of these guys ran into many disasters alongside the manner however they did not allow this to forestall them. They re-tested the situation after failure, went decrease back in and studies and researched and discovered how they will make it better and exchange the present day situation. They perfected their demanding situations and got here decrease returned stronger and higher than ever. That is what it takes for all of us to truly grow to be wealthy and get what it's miles they may be looking for out of this existence. You can't be fearful of failure, as an opportunity use it as an possibility.

You can not circulate into topics blindly. You must be willing to investigate and acknowledged statistics and figures of the problem. You ought to apprehend that it takes a sturdy commitment and a choice to want to get up to now in lifestyles and additionally you need to be willing to make a few sacrifices along the way. The sort of sacrifices will variety, however you inclined to undergo them and apprehend that they may be handiest going that will help you in the end.

Chapter 22: Getting Rich: The Bottom Line
With the statistics supplied here we hope that you have been able to discover belief and idea to make it to the top. We additionally desire you have decided out what it takes to make it to the pinnacle and that it is actually an opportunity that may be your in case you are willing to move that

extra mile to get it. Anyone can do it, however such a lot of are ignorant of what to do to get there. Now you've got that data firsthand.

If you are organized to come to be wealthy and overlook all the issues that existence can bring, it's miles it gradual to polish and the opportunity is now to your fingers. If you can perform a little component with that possibility now is the time to obtain out and get it.

Here are the steps that you need to take to make it to the pinnacle and get rich.

1.Know what you want, the quantity of coins that you need and the way you could get it.

2.Write all your thoughts out on paper. List what you need to do and the manner you will do that.

3.Find a economic adviser.

four.Change the manner that you think and recognize that in case you want it you can get it with the proper attempt.

five.Never give up. There can be stressful situations that come along however the ones stressful conditions are all things that you can overcome so long as you in no way surrender.

Becoming wealthy is some detail that you can do. Anyone can do it. If you're ready to turn out to be rich and trade the manner which you live all the time, all it takes is the proper mindset and placing your words into movement.

www.ingramcontent.com/pod-product-compliance
Lightning Source LLC
Chambersburg PA
CBHW071220210326
41597CB00016B/1889